Lester Pearson leads Liberals to victory in federal election.

W. V. O'Neill killed by FLQ bomb explosion in Montreal.

The Neptune in Halifax and the Playhouse in Vancouver begin their first theatrical seasons.

Real Caouette becomes head of Quebec Creditiste Party after split with Social Credit Party.

Aujourd'hui...
c'est l'électricité

La préposée aux renseignements

Accueillante, attentive, prévenante, elle est toujours heureuse de vous rendre service. Que vous désiriez un renseignement au sujet de votre facture, d'un déménagement ou de toute autre chose, consultez-la en tout temps. Elle est à votre disposition pour vous aider à obtenir le meilleur service possible.

Q   Hydro-Québec

Hydro Québec takes over 11 private power companies.

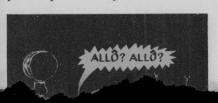

ALLÔ? ALLÔ?

LESTER PEARSON AND NUCLEAR WARHEADS

"A RIOT OF INDECISION"

OCTOBER. 1960– PAUL HELLYER
(LIBERAL DEFENCE SPOKESMAN)
SAINT JOHN TELEGRAPH JOURNAL

"The Bomarc missile is about the most useless expense of money you can devise. The Government might as well collect taxes and dump the money into Northumberland Strait."

AUGUST, 1960—LESTER B. PEARSON—
HOUSE OF COMMONS:

"In my view, we should get out of the whole SAGE-BOMARC operation."

Pearson and Kennedy sign nuclear warheads for BOMARC missiles pact.

Canada and Russia sign $500 million wheat deal.

Separatist demonstrations mar Montreal's Place des Arts opening.

Strike of 1,300 longshoremen shuts down St. Lawrence shipping.

Eleven FLQ terrorists draw 12-year maximum sentences for bombings.

TCA airliner crashes at Ste-Thérèse, Que., killing 118 passengers.

Trans-Pacific phone cable connects Australi... erni, B.C.

Construction begins on Deuterium of Canada heavy-water plant at Glace Bay, N.S.

Tidal wave from Alaska earthquake swamps B.C. coastal towns.

Lyall Dagg... ... wins world's curling title at Cal...

Northern Dancer wins Kentucky Derby.

Marshall McLuhan publishes *Understanding Media*.

Work begins on Great Canadian Oil Sands plant at Fort McMurray, Alta.

SIU ex-president Hal Banks skips bail after conspiracy sentence.

Texas Gulf Sulphur announcement of ore discoveries in Timmins, Ont., sparks trading of 16 million shares on New York Stock Exchange.

FIRST DAY COVER JULY 29, 1964

CHARLOTTETOWN CONFERENCE

Confederation Centre opening heads P.E.I.'s celebration of Charlottetown Conference centennial.

Quebec greets Queen with jeers and boos on Canadian tour.

CHUM

See PAUL & his

AUG. 17

The Beatles take No... ... by storm with concerts in Montreal, Toronto and Vancouver.

George Hungerford and Roger Jackson win gold medal in pairs rowing at Tokyo Olympics.

'Flag committee! What flag committee?'

Six-month flag debate ends with adoption of red maple leaf.

Yukon MP Eric Nielson shocks Commons with Rivard Affair exposé.

Canadian contingent sent to Cyprus with UN peacekeeping force.

Social Insurance Numbers become standard tax ID.

The Years of Protest

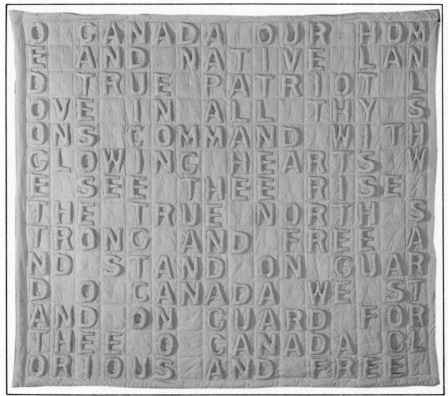

Intense, enigmatic, a moment frozen in time — New Brunswick artist Alex Colville painted Pacific, 1967 *while in California.*

Previous page: *Joyce Wieland's art turned "Patriotic-Pop" in the '60s, with assemblages like her famous* O Canada *quilt.*

Alan Edmonds
The Years of Protest
1960/1970

Canada's Illustrated Heritage

Canada's Illustrated Heritage

Publisher: Jack McClelland
Editorial Consultant: Pierre Berton
Historical Consultant: Michael Bliss
Editor-in-Chief: Toivo Kiil
Associate Editors: Michael Clugston
Clare McKeon
Harold Quinn
Jean Stinson
Assistant Editor: Marta Howard
Design: William Hindle
Lynn Campbell
Neil Fraser Cochrane
Cover Artist: Alan Daniel
Picture Research: Lembi Buchanan
Michel Doyon
Betty Gibson
Christine Jensen
Margot Sainsbury

ISBN: 0-9196-4428-7

N.S.L. Natural Science of Canada Limited
254 Bartley Drive
Toronto, Ontario M4A 1G1

Printed and bound in Canada

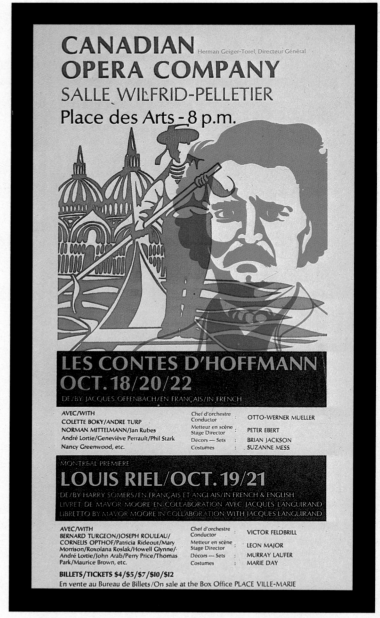

The Canadian Opera Company's 1967 Montreal premiere of Harry Somers' Louis Riel *drew thunderous applause. Four years before, separatists had picketed the opening of the Place des Arts.*

Contents

A Decade of Dizzying Changes

Man has reached out and touched the tranquil moon. Puisse ce haut fait permettre à l'homme de redécouvrir la terre et d'y trouver la paix. [*May that high achievement allow man to rediscover the earth and find peace.*]

Pierre Trudeau, Canada's message on the moon via *Apollo 11,* July 20, 1969

There were two islands in time known as the 1960s: one was the decade according to the calendar, January 1, 1960 to December 31, 1969; the other, "the 1960s," spanning both that decade and the early part of the 1970s. In that second sense "the 1960s" is an historical reference point, used in much the same way as, say, the Victorian Era or the Industrial Revolution. It's an appropriate comparison. We're still so close to the decade that judgments are perilous, but even so it does seem likely that "the 1960s" were of epochal significance in Canadian history.

What happened in the historical sixties is that the world changed. A great many issues that had been fermenting near the surface of society for twenty years or more erupted at more or less the same time. There was undreamed of affluence, and that meant survival for almost everyone was assured. This freed energies previously consumed by the task of staying alive. There was the gathering pace of the technological revolution which – under

the guise of automation – irrevocably changed the nature of work. People increasingly became the handmaidens of, or were replaced by, the machine. Sociologists and scientists began to realize the world was overpopulated. Women began to demand a new place in society – a place equal to man's. There was something called "the New Morality," not to mention a growing and assertive sense of nationalism. And there was the "Youthquake." Above all, there was the Youthquake.

All these forces and more trying to co-exist on the same island in time produced a whirlwind of eruptive, often disruptive, change. And while this change was most apparent during the core years of the historical sixties, it all began in the *real* sixties – the calendar decade.

At midnight on December 30, 1959, some average Canadian families sat down with what was still an obsessively new toy – the TV set – to watch a live telecast of the New Year and New Decade celebrations in Times Square, New York. They stayed at home partly because of the TV, and partly because in Canada most partying was still done there. The men wore suits with slim pants and long jackets. Their hair was cropped close; often it was no longer than the bristles on the brushes used by women on their own shoulder-length hair. Women's fashions, too, reflected the influence of elegant, modest yesterdays. They wore

Marshall McLuhan's Understanding Media *revolutionized language and thinking in the '60s: the world was a "global village" changing with mind-boggling speed in the wake of electronic communication.*

Opposite page: *According to media analysts, Lester Pearson's "what me worry" image was no match for "Dief the actor" when TV turned election campaigns into show-biz.*

The "beatniks" of the late '50s and early '60s were the first conspicuous "dropouts" from a society they saw as obsessed with money and status. Photographer John Max caught an artist-friend, Godfrey Stephens, adding a "beat" epitaph to his mural in this Montreal "pad" in 1961.

calf-length sack dresses which camouflaged their shapes, and their hair was "teased" or backcombed into a high, lacquered bouffant. To drink there was probably beer and rye-and-ginger, with Coke for the teenagers who, in their parents' company, respected the law that forbade drinking until age twenty-one.

In the recreation room in the basement (by 1960 it seemed most Canadians lived in the sort of house that included basement recreation rooms) there would be dancing, and the kids and the younger adults might have done the Twist, the new dance in which men and women didn't dance together but stood apart and wiggled their hips. The music came from the "hi-fi" and was fast and loud and not very melodic. Parents were prone to order it turned down, or off.

This book is about the dizzying changes that overtook this fairly typical Canadian family in the next ten years. Often, the stories involve the individuals who, in any age, stand out in a crowd and yell and attract attention. In this book we are often talking about people who attracted the attention of "the media" – of television and radio and newspapers and magazines. And that's appropriate, because to a great extent it was the media that was responsible for the speed of change. On television news a fad could become a trend, and a trend a fact – all within the space of a day. And all this had a profound effect on the nation, so that if we looked at that more or less average Canadian family ten years later . . .

. . . the TV was in colour, but even that was no longer a novelty, and the set had been relegated to the recreation room or den. There weren't as many happy family parties now, partly because there weren't as many happy families as there had been. The divorce rate was rising, and parents and kids viewed each other across what was already known as the "generation gap."

Men's hair was almost down to the collar and

worn with sideburns. For all that outraged some and prompted others to sneer, the shoulder-length locks of teenage boys and young men in their early twenties had made long hair fashionable, and most older men wore it at least over their ears. That also meant wearing pants with flared bottoms, like sailors' bell-bottoms. Women, particularly the younger ones, wore their hair long and straight, and if there was enough of it, they let it fall like a curtain alongside their faces. Skirts were thigh-high, as revealing as cheerleaders' dresses a decade earlier.

There was still rye-and-ginger to drink – and scotch and gin and vodka and rum and wine and perhaps even Pernod and Cointreau. Canadians became the world's most travelled people during the 1960s, and developed some taste for eating and drinking. The drinking age was still twenty-one, but most parents permitted the over-sixteens to drink on New Year's Eve – if they happened to be at home. Those in their late teens probably had taken the second car and gone out with friends.

For dancing the music came from the "stereo" – a sound system that looked as if it could fly you to the moon if you stumbled on the right buttons to push and knobs to twirl. The music itself was likely to be thunderously amplified and bear only a slight similarity to the Twist. It may have been "Cold Turkey," a cut from the album made in Toronto by international superstar John Lennon of the Beatles. The song had nothing to do with eating; the title described "kicking" drugs.

Canada was a joyous place that New Year's Eve in 1969. The pace of change had brought problems because no one could keep up with it: old unshakable truths had a habit of becoming quaint overnight. But materially Canadians had never had it so good. Indeed, by 1969 we had become so accustomed to the security that affluence had brought that we felt collectively free to question the status quo and protest that it needed

To a great extent it was Pierre Trudeau's radical image – his unconventional clothes; his off-the-cuff remarks; his liberal views on divorce, capital punishment, sex, marijuana; his trips to China and Russia; his physical fitness and "swinging" life – that wooed the youth vote in '68.

The introduction of DC-8 jets by Trans-Canada Airlines in 1960 cut flying time between Montreal and Vancouver from ten to six hours. A year later, Canadian Pacific (which had broken TCA's cross-continent monopoly in '59) inaugurated its own jet service and established eight-hour non-stop flights between Vancouver and London over the North Pole.

changing.

Much of the protest was noisy, and the focus of restlessness usually involved the young. Some protest, however, was more subtle and, at the time, not seen as such. The movement to restore old city-core houses and save them from apartment-block developers was, for instance, as significant a demand for change as students' violent demands for more power in the universities. So was the unprecedented number of strikes: in a significant number of cases the workers were merely protesting because they were paid less than their counterparts in the United States.

In fact by August, 1966, the Toronto *Globe and Mail* noticed a "curious mood of rebellion, of irresponsibility, of resentment, not perhaps clearly recognized but nevertheless expressed [in ways that show] Canadians are doubting all former stable things."

Well, as the decade ended three years later, we were still rich enough and secure enough to feel the same way. To those who knew how and where to look, there were signs of trouble in Paradise, but from where most Canadians sat the storm clouds were out of sight, and tomorrow promised to be as exciting as yesterday had been and today was.

The euphoria, the excitement, the unprecedented faith in tomorrow lasted until the end of the historical 1960s in fact. People who lived through the closing years of one decade and the start of the next thought of it all as the sixties, and it serves no purpose to remind them that such-and-such an event happened in 1971, or that a particular fad, fashion or piece of music dates from 1971, or 1972.

It is still too close for academic historians to pass judgment on the 1960s: too many people who experienced them are still alive to quarrel with their conclusions. However, of all the changes that the sixties brought about, at least two seem more durable than the rest.

The first was that women, when they confronted the change in their traditional role, demanded re-negotiation of the established relationships between the sexes. The women's liberation movement, born in the 1960s, had more impact on Canada than on other western nations: we were more recently a rural, agrarian nation and so, in 1960, Canadian men and women were more firmly fixed in traditional attitudes than most western people.

The second conclusion is, perhaps, so optimistic that it borders on being a hope. In 1969, it was an article of faith for youth that the "Establishment," the power brokers, and those who played politics would never again tell them what to do. Children born in the post World War II baby boom came of age, didn't like what they had inherited, and tried to change it. And in numbers they were so many that to a large extend it was this that was summed up in the words of a nineteen-year-old, who in 1969 fled north to Canada from the United States. He said:

It's mad. Even my own father wanted me to go. He said it was my duty to my country, as it was his duty to go off and fight the Japanese in the Second World War. You know, someone came along and ordered him: "Joe, you're the good guy and he's the bad guy and so off you go and kill him for us." I'll tell you, that won't happen again, not ever.

Despite Vietnam and a score of other mini-wars going on during the decade, the 1960s also produced the first generation that was not really "bloodied" by war. They were the generation that was told to fight one, and refused. The 1960s should have taught the power brokers and politicians that they have to do what the people want, or else. Optimistic? Perhaps. But then so were the sixties.

MARSHALL MCLUHAN, WHAT ARE YOU DOIN'? *was a common bit of graffiti on college washroom walls in the sixties — as much a demand for another prophecy from the "guru of mass communications" as a plea to have him leave well enough alone. Author of four best-selling books in the decade (The Gutenberg Galaxy, Understanding Media, The Medium is the Massage, and War and Peace in the Global Village), the University of Toronto professor became the oracle of a generation of advertising executives, teachers and politicians. Before his bid for the Liberal leadership, Pierre Trudeau paid McLuhan a visit.*

*Four hours on the Ten Commandments?
Any discourse on the subject in a
church or synagogue would have met
a sea of yawns. But not Cecil B.
DeMille's Hollywood version of the
book of Exodus. Rivers turning to
blood, plagues of locusts, a bush
going up in flames and the Red Sea
parting to the wave of Charlton
Heston's magic wand – all in Vista
Vision and Technicolor – were enough
to lure these slicked-down Montreal
teenagers to the movies in '66. All
that's missing is a couple of chicks
to share the popcorn in the balcony.*

CHAPTER ONE

The Comfortable Empty Pew

Of all the charges made against the Christian Church, in good times and bad, from within and without, there are two that seldom abate: the charges of smugness and self-righteousness.

Ralph Allen, "The Hidden Failure of Our Churches," *Maclean's,* February 25, 1961

Anne Spiller was not the stuff of which heroes are made. An ex-schoolmate described her as "average blah," which was unkind, but not entirely inaccurate. What she did was not exactly heroic in the traditional sense either. Between 1967 and 1969 Anne, then a bank teller of twenty-five, stole almost half a million dollars from the Penticton, British Columbia, branch of the Royal Bank of Canada.

She lived in a house with gold-plated door knobs, was learning to play her new $7,500 baby grand, and drove a Cadillac with so many extras the only thing it wouldn't do was fly. Occasionally she took friends on weekend jaunts to Hawaii, and once tipped her hairdresser with a diamond ring. When finally she came to trial, incredulous bank inspectors found she'd blown every penny of the stolen $492,000. And though she was jailed for three years, Anne Spiller's crime earned her the sneaking admiration, if not exactly the whole-hearted approval, first in her home town, and then across the nation.

When *Maclean's* magazine described her as being "as forgettable as all bank clerks and Eaton's salesgirls," there was a flood of protests – not from outraged citizens condemning the thief, but from a legion of bank clerks and Eaton's salesgirls angry at being called "forgettable."

In 1960, Anne Spiller would have been roundly condemned by an outraged Canada. But something drastic happened between 1960 and the day of Anne Spiller's trial one sunny morning in October 1968.

Some said the trouble was that God died around 1966. Others claimed simply that the 1960s youth explosion brought truth and honesty and destroyed hypocrisy. Most agreed that if God didn't actually die, the lifestyle He represented had begun to fall apart. The 1960s became the decade of the option: we were forever confronted with undreamed-of freedom of choice, whether we were buying a car or trying to decide on moral values. Somehow, a term known to ministers, rabbis and philosophers as "situation ethics" had come into common use.

As with everything in the sixties, the real upheavals didn't surface until the end of the decade, but even in 1960 there were straws in the wind. The province of Alberta finally permitted men and women to drink in the same bar, and plebiscites were planned on whether movies should be shown on Sundays in Toronto. As early as 1961, only ho-

The Comfortable Pew

A critical look at the Church in the New Age

Pierre Berton

Not only the Anglicans (who had commissioned the critical study) but Christian churches in general were "fit to be tied" when Pierre Berton launched his bombshell bestseller, The Comfortable Pew, *in 1965. Accusing the churches of being "mute followers, out of step with the times" and "guardians of temporal wealth in the face of spiritual poverty," the book sparked debates that still echo through church halls.*

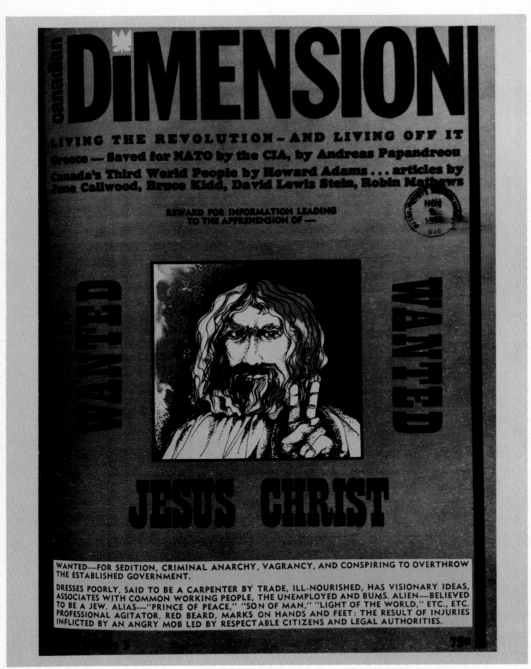

Jesus the Radical (which he was historically) became a kind of cult figure for some during the years of protest. Activists and "Jesus Freaks" saw his anti-establishment teachings as "right on."

tels in Nova Scotia were allowed to serve liquor, and only in Quebec could you buy a drink with meals on Sunday. In 1965, at a reception for visiting Soviet Deputy Premier Dmitri Polyansky, Ontario Premier John Robarts asked his guests to put down their drinks when being photographed. As Robarts explained to the puzzled Russian: "One Canadian custom is that we all drink but we don't want anyone to know we do." We still paid lip service to our traditional bedrock beliefs that to work was virtuous; to save a necessity; to respect authority a duty – and to actually enjoy Sundays quite sinful.

throwing caution to the winds

Affluence changed all that. Second only to the Americans, we were individually richer than we had ever been. That first became true during the 1950s when Canadians squirrelled away their money and established the national claim that no breed on earth had more money on deposit in savings accounts and insurance companies. In the 1960s, however, we threw caution to the winds.

Detroit cars were, as usual, the bellwether of both social attitudes and the economy. In Canada in 1959, for instance, Ford sold six models, all but one aimed at low and middle income buyers. By 1969, Ford offered twenty-three models, a third of them so luxurious they would have been labelled rich men's cars a few years earlier. One Ford publicity man claimed that by permutating options and models it was possible that every car made by the company could in some way be different from all the others. The range of choice was so staggering that it was hard for people to make up their minds.

Faith in the future had as much to do with affluence as real money. It seemed you could buy anything for nothing down and so much a month. Even banks competed to outlend one another. As a result the Allied Boating Association of Canada was able to report early in the decade that: "As with cars, the two-boat family is now fairly common," and the Chrysler Corporation summed up the climate with the slogan: "The Best Years Are Right Now." It was perhaps the first time in human history that ordinary people could afford to find out whether the grass on the other side of the fence really was greener.

In the midst of all this, Dr. Raymond Prince, a McGill University psychiatrist, reported that mental stress, nervous problems, sleeplessness, depression and general irritability were more common among the poor than among the well-off. Yes indeed, but who was "poor?" In Toronto in 1960, you couldn't claim welfare from the city if you had a television set, telephone or car. By January 1965, the Dominion Bureau of Statistics' list of basic commodities used to measure the cost of living included frozen foods, air travel, floor polishers, dishwashers and air conditioners. By the end of the decade, you could own your own house and still get welfare.

the death of God

Less noticeably, God began to show signs of terminal illness–or if not God exactly, then His established churches. Science *seemed* to be able to explain and control everything, so there was less need to explain mysteries as "acts of God."

It's true that in 1964, a county court turned down the citizenship bid of Mr. and Mrs. Ernest Bergsma of Caledonia, Ontario, because as atheists the Bergsmas refused to take an oath that ended with the words "So help me God." But as early as 1961 the Reverend Angus MacQueen, a former moderator of the United Church, was saying the church "is not doing a very creditable job ... she is too comfortable and too well-adjusted to the status quo." In 1965, a United Church survey

The Christian pavilion at Expo reflected the sharp shift in churches toward social concern, confronting the complacent with stark photos of starvation, prejudice, war, poverty and loneliness.

Revised Standard Versions

It seemed nothing was sacred anymore: radical churchmen crying "God is dead"; priests and nuns leaving to get married; schisms over the Latin Mass, birth control, the Virgin birth, the existence of the Devil, the creation of the world, the deity of Jesus . . . yes, even over ecumenism itself. Clergy and laity alike wondered what had happened to the boom in church building in the fifties, and why were Sunday schools no longer packed? Now half-empty sanctuaries were becoming "white elephants" for real estate agents to sell as would-be theatres or day care centres.

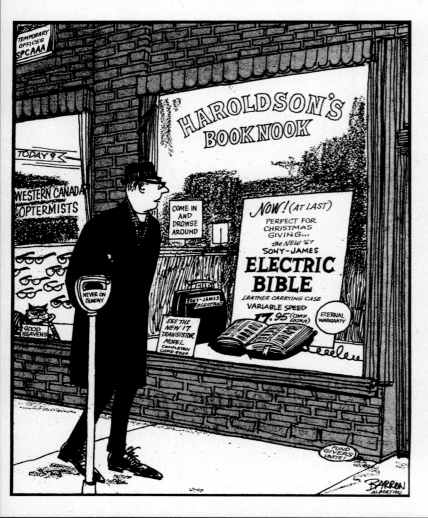

"We'll just have to give them Hell on Sunday."

"Until Christmas, then...?"

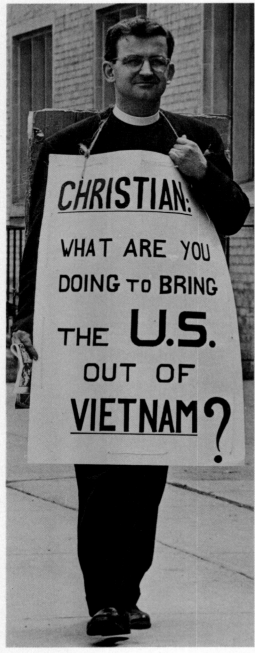

While TV brought the atrocities of the Vietnam war into everyone's living room, Rev. Dan Heap took his protest of Canada's complicity right to the Anglican Church House door in Toronto.

of 1,700 laymen and 347 ministers concluded that "traditional religious beliefs are breaking down faster than ever." And the church itself had already discarded some of those traditional beliefs; by then the United Church had abandoned its preaching of total abstinence and had formally decided there were two kinds of Christians – "those who practise total abstinence and those who practise temperate use."

wobbly foundations

Even the Ten Commandments came under attack. In *Honest to God*, the English bishop John Robinson claimed "the only intrinsic evil is the lack of love." Nothing was quite what it seemed any more. Even work, from which most people got a sense of accomplishment as well as an income, came to be questioned. It was often so automated and systemized it provided little sense of satisfaction. More and more products became "throwaway" and plastic, with a high degree of built-in obsolescence.

The traditional foundations of Canada were, then, a bit wobbly midway through the sixties. And it was then that the so-called "Youthquake" turned the country, along with most of the western world, on its ear. The post-World War II baby boom had grown up. By 1965, the advance guard was seventeen and eighteen, and suddenly a statistic became a catch phrase: *half the population is under twenty-five.* Graffiti – maxims of the counter-culture scrawled on bathroom walls – announced: "Never trust anyone over thirty." The parent generation of forty or more and the big brother generation between twenty-five and thirty-five virtually lost control. In the words of Bay Street investment expert Norman Short, society became "destabilized."

Part of the problem now was the affluent society was a little unsure of itself. When journalist and TV personality Pierre Berton published his 158-page book *The Comfortable Pew* in January 1965, he concluded that the Anglican Church had been either silent or "weak, tardy, equivocal and irrelevent" when faced with the great issues of the time. These issues included "the whole contemporary question of business morals, the tensions between industry and labour, the sexual revolution that has changed the attitudes of the western world."

Berton drew sharp aim when he raised the subject of the sexual revolution. In this matter, he wrote: "Church leaders are woefully behind the times and it is safe to say that large numbers of them do not know what is happening or do not want to believe it when they are told."

the game of Divorce

But what could older generations say on the subject of sex? They weren't doing so well themselves. Fifties marriages seemed to go bust with the frequency of balloons at a New Year's Eve party. With new affluence, couples could *afford* the luxury of splitting up. One of the popular games was Divorce, which involved a Monopoly-like board with squares marked "Your First Fight" and "Leave Home and Go Back to Mother."

By the end of the decade, the Universities of Manitoba and Saskatchewan handed freshman students information kits entitled: "The Pill, Abortion and VD–How To Handle Them." In Winnipeg in 1960, male contraceptives could legally be sold only to prevent disease. By 1968, a general practitioner in the Winnipeg suburb of St. James reported that one set of comfortably middle-class parents had asked him to prescribe the birth-control pill for their daughter of fourteen "to save us worrying." It was, the GP claimed, to avoid responsibility for their own child's morality.

Pierre Berton wrote in *The Comfortable Pew*:

Last year, the good ladies of the Church of the Ascension ran off all their own parish lists, vestry minutes and Sunday bulletins on a Gestetner Stencil Duplicator.
They saved themselves $1,122.08.

Maybe you should be running things yourself too.

When the Reverend Canon Thompson first came to Toronto from Truro, N.S., his newly assigned parish had no books, no money and no place to worship.

So he started knocking on doors. And nineteen months later they had a church.

"It was tough going at first," said the Canon, "we had to watch where every single penny went. That's why we got a Gestetner."

A Gestetner salesman had explained how they could save up to 40% on printing costs and still get professional looking work.

"It's so important to have things done nicely for the church," said Mrs. Ruth Griffin, who, along with Mrs. Maureen Morris prints up everything from the bazaar flyers to an impressive 25-page annual report. "But to have a printer do all our work would have cost us a fortune."

"We're getting professional results just the same," said Canon Thompson, "thanks to my ladies and their Gestetner. And just look at all the money we're saving!"

"You might say," he added with a wink, "Gestetner was the answer to our prayers." Maybe you should be running things yourself too. Write, Gestetner, 849 Don Mills Road, Don Mills, Ont. And get started.

Gestetner
The people who can help you run things yourself

Ferment '68, *an inter-faith journal headed by an advisory board of Jews, Muslims, Buddhists, Catholics and Protestants of every stripe, had advertisers tailor their ads to the faithful.*

Rundle Memorial (named after the first Methodist missionary in the Edmonton area) was among the many churches that tried to keep pace with affluent, sometimes apathetic parishioners: relaxed dress, short services, and sermon topics that would warm the heart of a golden calf. Downstairs, a weekend coffee house called The Unsquare Cellar tried to compete with night clubs in the city's gaslight district. In Vancouver, one minister staged a rock band and go-go dancer for its youth service. Unamused older members had the pastor censured.

"if man has truly come of age he no longer needs the father figure of a God." Perhaps not, but he clearly needed something. In 1960 there were six hundred psychiatrists practising in Canada. In 1969 there were twelve hundred. In 1968 Ouija boards were outselling Monopoly games, closely followed by the game ESP, and books on reincarnation and psychic phenomena outsold the Bible. One community college in Toronto ran an evening course in witchcraft.

Mood-changing drugs were also seen as a route to salvation. A middle-aged Harvard psychologist, Dr. Timothy Leary, acquired the status of a cult hero because he defended the use of hallucinogens (from pot to LSD) on the grounds that they were mind-expanding and induced religious experiences. The fundamentalist churches – those that preached a simple good *versus* evil or God *versus* the devil Christianity – flourished, and sometimes they bought up vacant churches that the ailing denominational churches had abandoned.

New forms of salvation presented themselves too. The word *guru* (Hindu for spiritual leader) entered the language, and we imported many a *guru* from the east. The most famous was the Maharishi Mahesh Yogi, who advocated trancendental meditation from his headquarters alongside the River Ganges, in Rishikesh, three hours from New Delhi. Like most of the so-called mystics, his message was appealingly simple: "You are God and God is You." In 1968, Paul Saltzman, a nineteen-year-old Canadian film maker, returned starry-eyed from a pilgrimage to Rishikesh and reported: "In the language of Christianity, the Maharishi is really teaching something like those Ten Commandments that talk about loving thy neighbour and the meek inheriting the earth."

Equally popular as a source of salvation was the Church of Scientology, founded by a former science fiction writer, L. Ron Hubbard, who maintained his headquarters aboard a yacht that was constantly at sea. In an age when humans viewed computers and electronic technology with suspicious awe, Scientology was appropriately based on the print-outs of machines called E-meters. Acolytes paid hundreds of dollars for the privilege of passing through five levels of "liberation" from the prejudices and bigotry of western society.

In an attempt to end their unhealthy separation from emotion, people flocked to "encounter groups," which began (as so much of the sixties did) in California and were brought north by psychologist Frederick Perls, when he set up shop in Vancouver. The encounter group consisted of perhaps a dozen people who spent anywhere up to a week together, closeted during their waking hours in one room, probing one another's innermost thoughts and feelings, trying to ferret out the truth behind each other's actions and words. Spiritualism enjoyed renewed popularity; something called psycho-cybernetics was touted as a new cure-all; and astrology flourished so that in Toronto a computer was programmed to produce print-out horoscopes at $15 or $25 a time. There was freedom for everyone to pursue happiness in his or her unique way, by "doing your own thing."

The Youthquake had created a social climate in which "ripping off the system" was one alternative to working. In the winter of 1969, the Unemployment Insurance Commission investigated 116,010 claims and found 24,486 to be fraudulent, costing about $9 million a year. Benefit cheques were sometimes forwarded to places like Mexico or Florida. One man from Timmins, Ontario, lived in sunny Italy, while his family mailed him his pogey payments.

It was in such a climate that Anne Spiller was found with her hand in the till of the bank where she worked. As her hairdresser commented: "I don't see what all the fuss is about. I mean it was only money belonging to a big fat bank, after all."

Man Without God

The pronouncement "God is Dead" was nothing new, of course: atheists had been saying that for a century, ever since the German philosopher Friedrich Nietzsche published his famous obituary condemning modern man for the murder. Whether he was a prophet or a heretic didn't really matter. More important was the fact that the denominational churches were half-empty, considered bankrupt, if not by the banks, then certainly by many members who only "warmed a pew" at Easter, Christmas and christenings. And what were to be the consequences of a godless society? As dire as anything envisioned by artist William Kurelek in his painting *Behold, Man Without God* (right). And how did organized religion try to meet the challenge? Some congregations directed their outreach programmes toward social problems. Some, notably orthodox Jews and fundamentalist Christians, saw compromise and accommodation as a symptom of moral decay and went back to the basics – and claimed converts by the thousands. And the back-sliders? Some filled their spiritual voids with new doctrines, new messiahs, astrology, drug-induced "highs" and shady experiences that offered the promise of "self-actualization." If the "God of our fathers" was dead, there were plenty of alternates on the market waiting to be embraced.

Alberta-born William Kurelek, the son of immigrant parents and a convert to Roman Catholicism, painted Behold, Man Without God *in the early sixties – an indictment of greedy, self-centred mankind. In its surrealistic tones and symbology, the work depicts the effects of modern man's courtship of the "Seven Deadly Sins."*

The Underground Press

In Vancouver its was *Georgia Straight,* in Winnipeg *Omphalos,* in Toronto, *Harbinger,* in Ottawa *Octopus,* and in Montreal *Logos*—all of them billed as "Free Press" papers, each tied into the continent-wide Underground Press Syndicate. The editors and workers were mostly volunteers, kids from middle-class homes who, a few years before, had written for the high school newspaper and headed the student council. Yet, here they were, pecking out articles on the revolutionary of the month, reviews of rock concerts, "be-ins" and "love-ins," exposés of narcs and cops and war-mongering politicians, and reports based on street-talk of the quality, prices and supplies of drugs. The ads were all "hip" and the classified all "groovy"; the art "eastern psychedelic" and comics all about the "pothead's" hassles with "the man."

Georgia Straight *editors were back in court when this August '68 issue went to press, this time for "criminal libel against a magistrate."*

Printed in the shadow of Ottawa's Peace Tower, Octopus *features for 1968-69 included "Cop as Pig," "Demonstrations Help" and "Revolution?"*

Harbinger's *front page for October 1, 1969: the staff-artist's "pipe-dream." Reviewed: Toronto's September Insanity Street Festival.*

Considering the grab-bag contents of most early underground papers, it's not surprising that all except Georgia Straight *folded before the decade's end. Like many communes, started in a spirit of "freedom and love," they simply collapsed when there was rent to pay or joe-jobs to be done. Commercial "rip-off artists" were already moving in on the hip-clothing, rock-music and health-food scene, as a new "alternate press" paper,* Guerilla, *reported in June 1970.*

MICHAEL BUTLER PRESENTS

HAIR
THE AMERICAN TRIBAL-LOVE ROCK MUSICAL

BOOK & LYRICS: GEROME RAGNI, JAMES RADO/MUSIC: GALT MACDERMOT
EXECUTIVE PRODUCER: BERTRAND CASTELLI/DIRECTED BY: TOM O'HORGAN
DANCE DIRECTOR: JULIE ARENAL
COLOUR BY BISHOP   COSTUMES: NANCY POTTS/SCENERY: ROBIN WAGNER/LIGHTING: JULES FISHER   COPYRIGHT © NATOMA PRODUCTIONS, INC.

IN ASSOCIATION WITH GLEN-WARREN PRODUCTIONS
ROYAL ALEXANDRA THEATRE
260 KING STREET WEST • TORONTO • PHONE: 363-4211

The opening of Hair – *"The American Tribal-Love Rock Musical" – at Toronto's Royal Alex in December 1969 may have heralded "the dawning of the Age of Aquarius" (as the overture's lyrics proclaimed), but most of the theatre's subscription-patrons had a hard time swallowing the show's "harmony and understanding, sympathy and trust abounding" message. It took almost a year of deliberation before the musical, scored by Montreal-born Galt MacDermot, had its Canadian premiere, and despite the advanced warning, some of the audience still stomped out over the language of some numbers. Those who stayed could hardly believe this was happening in "Toronto the Good" when members of the all-Canadian cast started taking off their clothes (albeit behind a heavy, gauze drapery) during the play's semi-nude orgy scene.*

CHAPTER TWO

Youthquake

Today's young people have too much materially and too little spiritually. They are beseiged with movies, television, magazines, books extolling sex and the fast life, yet when they become involved in this glamourized existence they are immoral.

Simma Holt, *Sex and the Teen-age Revolution*, 1967

In 1961, when the Youthquake kids would have been ten or younger, a Toronto teacher asked her grade four class to write an essay on the world they lived in and the future. All mentioned the Bomb, life in a fallout shelter, and the possible ways the world would end. It suddenly made sense that the young were afraid of inheriting their parents' world and seemed hell-bent on creating a new one of their very own. Not many of them could define this new world, but they all knew what it wasn't. It wasn't anything like the one the parent generation had created; a world in which humanity lived with the prospect of instant global annihilation, *and accepted the fact.*

What mattered in that crazy, mixed-up decade was not so much that the young rejected the values their parents held dear. After all, pressure for change has always come from the young, but historically they were never before powerful enough to force their issues. What did matter was that by the end of the decade people under twenty-five

were so numerous they represented an irresistible force—a massive bulge of energy in the social structure that the Establishment seemed unable to harness and use to its own ends. The young did not, as they had as recently as the fifties, represent a subculture. Instead, they created what came to be known as a counter-culture.

Ideally, this counter-culture would have been an alternative to that which already existed. In fact, it emerged more as a protest against virtually every symbol and value the parent generation held dear. The young rejected, but did not offer replacements. And so the decade ended in chaos, and though few dared try to define the shape of the future, one thing seemed fairly certain: for better or worse, the world would never be quite the same again.

It had all begun at the start of the decade, when the advance guard of the post-World War II baby boom was too young to make much impact on anyone except the Good Humor Man and kiddies' shoe stores. Two million babies were born in Canada between 1945 and 1948 and so by 1960, there were more teenagers around than ever. Measured against the young of forty years ago, boys of fifteen were four inches and girls two inches taller, and British biologist J. J. Tanner reported: "The world trend continues unabated, with Canada showing a somewhat greater rate of growth than other nations."

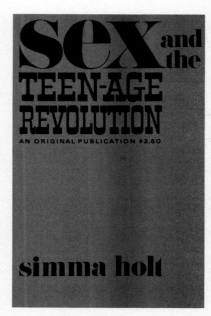

Vancouver Sun *columnist Simma Holt (later a Liberal* MP*) interviewed over 500 teenagers, groping for an explanation to the youth revolution. Published in '67, and peppered with first-hand accounts of sex, drugs, drinking, crime and broken families, the book offered parents no solution but to try to turn back the clock.*

One irate reader called The Panic Button *"vulgar, dirty, in poor taste, and a corruptor of youth,"* high praise for one of Toronto's first four-letter-word, underground magazines of the '60s.

Given a clearly defined issue such as the civil rights movement espoused by American students, it's possible that Canadian youth would have poured their energies into a specific cause early in the decade. In fact, at that time they spent their vigour on charming eccentricities that threatened no one, certainly not the status quo.

beatniks at The Garbage Pail

True, there were a few highly visible rebels known as beatniks – mostly scruffy characters who read poetry aloud at espresso coffee houses like The Garbage Pail in Montreal, the House of Hambourg in Toronto, the Yardbird Suite in Edmonton and The Question Mark in Vancouver. But for others the most outrageous activity was bed pushing. An extension of the phone-booth-cramming, goldfish-swallowing campus capers of the fifties, the aim was to see who could push a bed the farthest. Students at the University of British Columbia pushed a bed in their spare time for a month and logged 42 miles; but by mid-1961 Dalhousie University in Halifax had logged 350 miles and vanquished all comers, no one taking seriously the University of Toronto claim to 1,000 miles in a week of twenty-four hour pushing.

Meanwhile, the parent generation was obsessed with its own affairs – newer and bigger houses and basement-to-bedroom broadloom, second cars, dishwashers, and deciding whether ten- and twenty-year old marriages were worth saving. Thus it didn't at first notice the changes that would, within a few years, totally disrupt its way of life.

Among the army of the young, growing yearly as the first-born of the wartime baby boom reached the age of awareness, those changes were cataclysmic. They called themselves "bomb babies" who "grew up with fallout in our milk." Those between eighteen and twenty-five seemed to fall into two groups – the hippies and the activists. And early in the decade, they began to rock the boat . . . gently at first but from both sides.

The hippies were easiest to see, and so became better known. Hippies were successors to beatniks; sometimes it seemed that only the name changed. Hippies probably never totalled more than a fragment of the total generation, but they were pacesetters of protest, at least in style, to the sixteen-year-olds standing in the wings. Hippies were untidy, sometimes dirty, allegedly promiscuous. They wore round rimless "granny glasses," smoked marijuana cigarettes, and wore clothes that looked like rejects from the Salvation Army, and often were. They disapproved of anything favoured by "straights," (parents and almost everyone else) and moved constantly among their ghettos in Vancouver (the West 4th Avenue area), Toronto (the so-called Yorkville Village, an instant bohemia hidden by smart Bloor Street shop fronts), and Montreal.

hippies in transit

Cecilie Kwiat, who was twenty or so at the time, was in transit between Yorkville and West Fourth when she was found planting marijuana seeds alongside the Trans-Canada highway just east of Regina. "Saskatchewan needs *something*," she explained. She was very proud to be a hippie, and to have been a regular visitor to the throne room of the hippie kingdom, the Haight-Ashbury district of San Francisco. She explained the philosophy thus:

We start by feeling curiosity about something, about the country maybe – it's so big – and we travel and the curiosity turns into dissatisfaction and a kind of contempt for all that man has done.

On the other side of the social boat were the activists. They cared. The activists had short hair and

Friday and Saturday night audiences at Toronto's Yorkville coffee house "hootenannies" saw Ian and Sylvia (above), Gordon Lightfoot and other singers in concert before their first LPs.

Hysterical fans in Vancouver tried to break through the barricades just to touch John, Paul, George or Ringo. Incredulous parents, of course, couldn't fathom why their kids had gone nuts. Remember the "Beatles are Bugs" button?

The Beatles' first big hit in 1963, "She Loves You," rocketed the mop-top four from Liverpool, England, to international stardom with sell-out concerts wherever they went. This CHUM *Chart for May 9, 1966 had The Mamas & The Papas' single, "Monday, Monday" at the top of the list, but teens already bitten by the "Beatlemania" bug were already saving their allowance for the big event at the Gardens in Toronto.*

didn't worship marijuana. They were less visible and therefore less publicized, but they didn't like the world they had inherited either. Some founded the Canadian University Services Overseas (CUSO) in 1961 to send the energetic young to help deserving people in other countries, while other activists –particularly those in Quebec–found the focus for their discontent at home.

By 1965, then, there were two groups of malcontent young, ready to harness the enormous energy of the main body of the baby boom. Cecilie Kwiat and the other hippies wanted to "drop out" of the world, while the activists wanted to change it. By now the activists were teaching in high schools and universities. Toronto high school teacher Ann Shilton, who was thirty-five, explained: "We have a lot of younger teachers encouraging radicalism, some deliberately and some just because they see themselves as part of a great revolution."

Others saw such teachers as part of the Red Menace that had haunted the 1950s. In condemning "radical" teachers, Beth Wood, mayor of New Westminster, told an approving Vancouver Kiwanis Club: "If I don't want smallpox I don't go near people who have it. If we don't want communism we shouldn't let it be taught to our young."

What Mrs. Wood and the rest of the Establishment wanted was the sort of well-mannered obedience they themselves had offered to *their* parents and to the system. That way the older generation could stay in control. But those who could read the signs began to see what they were in for.

In the fall of 1965, the administration of Bayview Junior High in suburban Toronto posted the following regulation for behaviour in the halls:

All classes should begin lining up one minute before

Motorcycle gangs, like this troupe of "easy riders" roaring down Montreal's Dorchester Blvd., still raised hell and havoc at times but just didn't seem as menacing or strange after long-haired hippies became common on main streets.

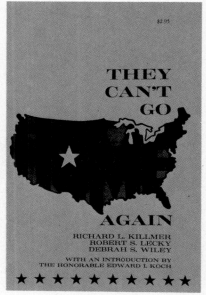

$2.95

THEY
CAN'T
GO
AGAIN

RICHARD L. KILLMER
ROBERT S. LECKY
DEBRAH S. WILEY

WITH AN INTRODUCTION BY
THE HONORABLE EDWARD I. KOCH

★ ★ ★ ★ ★ ★ ★ ★ ★ ★

An estimated 30,000 American youths dodging the military draft found their way to Canada before 1970, aided by U.S. resistance groups and organizations such as Toronto's Anti-Draft Programme. Many came via a modern version of the "Underground Railroad" of pre-Civil War days, and were amazed to find Canada welcomed them. Congressman Ed Koch (later mayor of New York) who contributed the introduction to They Can't Go Home Again, *had high praise to offer the Canadian government after his fact-finding interviews with evaders.*

the bell . . . girls will line up first in double file, and the boys behind them . . . classes should be ready for dismissal at the bell . . . should move into the halls in double file keeping as close as possible to the lockers on their right . . . noise, visiting en route, going to washrooms, drinking fountains and lockers shall not be permitted.

The name of the first martyr to rules of this kind is lost to history. It was almost certainly a boy dismissed for wearing his hair over his ears – a "Prince Valiant" haircut, they called it – in the style introduced by the Beatles. Neatly barbered principals kicked out scores of students and demanded they get haircuts. Older teachers were particularly bewildered. In New Westminster, British Columbia, a teacher set about reprimanding a girl for using the boys' washroom, and then discovered that she was a he.

As it turned out, the length and tidiness of hair – male hair, at least – was an important symbol for the Youthquake: the longer and shaggier the hair, the more rebellious they were – and the more violent and repressive was the Establishment's response.

The parent generation didn't approve of long hair, so it was therefore admirable. Anything, in fact, that "grossed out" (that is, offended) parents became high style. In 1966, there was a big market for replicas of the Iron Cross, the German army's highest award for valour, which some young people wore around their necks. The horrors of Nazi Germany and World War II were fresh in the minds of parents, and this was a particular outrage. John Leddy, then nineteen and one of four teenagers who shared a room in Toronto's Yorkville, wore his replica medal "to see how it bugs people because I got nothing against the Jews

Protests against the Vietnam War and Canada's arms sales became the campus cause. At U of T, picketers tried to evict recruiters for Dow Chemical (a napalm producer) during job interviews.

but, man, they give you dirty looks."

If you were young you either wore fashions that were unfashionable (old jeans or jeans made to look old; army surplus overcoats; dresses grandma would have liked), or fashions that only the young were equipped to wear (skirts so short, colours so vivid, pants and sweatshirts so tight that only lean, lithe young bodies looked good in them). By now, and simply by force of numbers, the baby boom bulge was setting the pace for the rest of society. To be young was to be where the action was. The slightly older generation that had grown up in the 1950s tried jumping on the bandwagon. Older women, who shouldn't have, wore mini-skirts and their husbands bellied out over wide belts and skin-tight jeans. Many smoked marijuana – which was always called something else, like grass or pot or tea or stuff – or pretended to. In the early days of its child-like innocence, the Youthquake was committed to the belief that love conquers all, and that formed the basis of the flower power movement that led to sidewalks and walls and cars everywhere being painted with multicoloured flowers.

Beatlemania

And then there was the music. Early on, the music was made mostly by the Beatles, a quartet of working-class English boys who wore their hair long over the forehead and played electronically amplified rock 'n' roll, which was loud and cacophonous and incomprehensible to the parent generation. Later, with the prescience of hindsight, University of Toronto sociologist Dr. Norman Bell would say we could have predicted the chaos if "we had just listened to the music."

Beatles' music was so violently different from anything that had gone before that the sound itself was a form of protest. The lyrics weren't, at least not at first. A typical million-selling early hit was called "I Wanna Hold Your Hand." In the early sixties, "Beatlemania" was a world-wide phenomenon. In 1965, the London office of Beatle Fan Clubs International announced that Canada had more card-carrying Beatlemaniacs than any other nation, Britain included. More than 50,000 Canadian kids had paid their dues.

By mid-decade, however, Beatles' style moon-in-June songs seemed a little old fashioned, particularly in the pace-setting United States where the young were finding that flower power wasn't enough to change the world. Above all, it did not end American involvement in the war in Vietnam. In fact, by June 1965, Washington admitted its troops were actually fighting with the South Vietnamese against communist guerillas.

drug-culture

As the draft swept up hundreds of thousands of boom babies to feed the Vietnam war, flower power gave way to a bitter resignation; to a period of rebellious disillusionment. Coincidentally pop music began to celebrate the birth of a so-called "drug culture" and the spread of a new morality. The new superstars were also from Britain. In lifestyle and song The Rolling Stones flaunted and lauded drug use and casual sex. Radio stations often banned their songs, and more would have been banned had it always been possible to make out the words.

By now, of course, even the Beatles had changed their tune. They, too, sang about casual sex and drugs, but you had to be young to know that "Lucy in the Sky With Diamonds" was the description of a "trip" on mood-changing drugs. A weedy youth with a nasal voice so highly pitched it was almost a whine, Bob Dylan was the poet and prophet of the counter-culture. As such he poured out all the sneering, pitying contempt the young felt for their elders in "Ballad of a Thin Man." It

Runaway teenagers usually thumbed their way to cities and "crashed" at a new-found friend's "pad" or a commune. Broke and hungry, their plea to passers-by was "Got any spare change?"

SIX ÉTUDIANTS NOUS EXPLIQUENT POURQUOI ILS FUMENT DE LA MARIJUANA

Widespread use of marijuana among the young (and adults too) prompted Châtelaine's *Montreal editors to ask* CEGEP *students the reason why. Under gouvernment sponsorship, the* Le Dain Commission *was asking the same questions at the same time.*

was about journalists and businessmen and parents who didn't know what was happening beneath the surface in the society at large.

What was "happening" was "hard" drugs. By now everyone knew about marijuana, and smoking it had even become fashionable among those who wished they were young. It was occasionally served instead of liquor at middle-class cocktail parties, and a hostess on Vancouver's elite Angus Drive even offered marijuana cigarettes from a cigarette box of inlaid ivory. She had them carefully rolled by a machine that also inserted a filter tip. But marijuana was a "soft" drug. "Uppers," "downers," and "acid" were considered the hard drugs.

"Uppers," included amphetamines which stimulated the nervous system; "downers" were barbiturates which calmed it; and "acid" or LSD altered perceptions to the point where the user totally escaped from reality.

"turn on, tune in, drop out"

Vancouver's *Georgia Straight,* the best known of the counter-culture's "underground" newspapers, once ran a "how-to" article on taking an LSD trip that read like a travel magazine's handy guide to vacationing in Europe. LSD was, at first anyway, not illegal, and a psychologist on the staff of Harvard University in Boston named Timothy Leary had promoted its use and that of similar drugs with the slogan: "Turn on, tune in, drop out." That is, the forty-year-old Leary invited the young to "turn on" to what was happening, to "tune in" to the energy of the universe, and to "drop out" of a society that wasn't worth belonging to. Harvard fired him.

Not all the young "dropped" acid, of course, or "popped" amphetamines and barbiturates, or availed themselves of the sexual freedoms of the counter-culture philosophy. Toronto's Yorkville

Village became Canada's so-called "hippie capital" and in the summer evenings of the dying years of the decade its half-dozen block-long streets seethed with crowds of kids cruising between coffee bars and rock clubs, occasionally taking part in ugly confrontations with "the man" (police). But, Cinderella-like, many of them went home to the suburbs come midnight.

psychedelic make-up

Even so, the use of drugs became so widespread that it changed the look of the world. The word used to describe the wildly coloured and weirdly distorted images induced by hallucinogens was "psychedelic," and by 1968, there were psychedelic posters, clothing, graphic design and face make-up.

In several cities–most notably in Toronto, Montreal and Vancouver–there were mobile clinics in the streets with staff trained in handling people having "bum trips" or "freaking out" on LSD or some other hallucinogen. In mid-decade, the federal government had set up and funded an organization called the Company of Young Canadians, designed to harness the energy and idealism of the young. By 1969, the CYC offered the footloose young a service which it advertised in Canadian newspapers this way:

Just got into town? Got no bread? Kicked out of your room? Got busted? Pregnant? Need Welfare? Freaking? Need legal advice? On a bummer? Hassled by the man? Need a job? Call Us.

There was a glorious paradox in all this: the counter-culture didn't have to waste its energy worrying about who would foot the bill for its activities; money was readily available from welfare and unemployment insurance and parents. Like the rest of western society, the system the young wanted to rip apart had made Canada rich enough to help finance the revolution that threatened to destroy it.

At this point in the Youthquake it didn't much matter that In English Canada the young lacked a focal issue for rebellion. The counter-culture explosion was global in scope, and eighteen-year-olds in Lethbridge and Prince Rupert and Digby could vicariously be part of student riots in France, in Germany, in Czechoslovakia, as well as in the United States. They, too, festooned bedroom walls with poster portraits of counter-culture idol Ché Guevara, the Cuban revolutionary.

Closest to home, American involvement in the war in Vietnam was the big issue. The war ended the era of flower power and caused widespread disillusionment among the young. It later put an end to apathy; it was the issue that "turned off" the drug culture. By 1967 there were almost 500,-000 American troops in Vietnam, and more than 14,000 had been killed. By 1969, that death toll was up to 33,641 plus seemingly countless casualties. Worse, American troops and their South Vietnamese allies were known to have committed atrocities among the peasants. The young everywhere began to see Vietnam as a threat to their generation, and anti-war demonstrations became bloody riots on college campuses and, bloodiest of all, in Chicago during the 1968 Democratic convention. Thus the decade ended with the Youthquake exploding into angry protest.

Typically, of course, the protest was more violent in the United States than here. When students mounted an anti-war demonstration outside the American embassy in Ottawa they were so quiet and orderly that nobody inside the building realized there had been a demonstration until they read the papers next morning. In Canada, the young reserved their most energetic protests for an issue that, on the surface, seemed far less explosive than Vietnam – education.

Button Power

Buttons – portable graffiti – made is easy to state your shtick *without a soapbox and get the point across at a glance in elevators, buses and subways.* STAMP OUT IMPORTS, EXPORTS AND LAMPORTS *was a Toronto button, attacking Mayor Allan Lamport for trying to clean out the city's hippies.*

Voices of Protest

How the pop music explosion in Canada got its start, and who the first real promoters behind it were, are questions no two people answer alike. But all will agree that it happened in the sixties, and that the beginnings were frustrating. While radio stations blared out *Billboard* magazine's top forty, and record stores kept pushing the same discs the DJs were playing, Canadian singers and bands were doing weekend "gigs" at $25 and $50 a night. Even if somebody put up the money to cut a single, most programme directors dismissed it as "homegrown junk." But not everybody did, and by the time Ian & Sylvia, Gordon Lightfoot, Joni Mitchell, Buffy Sainte-Marie, Neil Young, Davd Clayton-Thomas, Ann Murray, The Guess Who, The Stampeders . . . had hits selling well over 100,000 copies, no one had to ask what good could come from Canada. They knew.

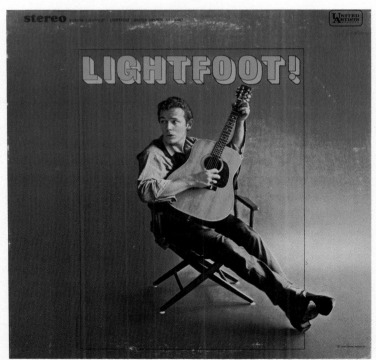

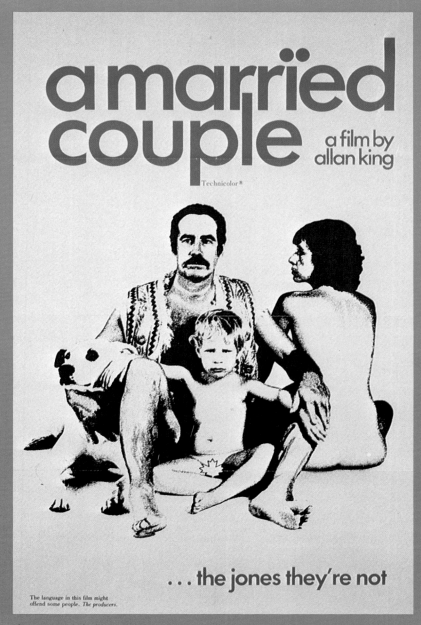

Goodbye Rose Marie! *Hello* Valerie! *In 1968, Montreal film director Denis Héroux moved camera and crew from bedroom to bedroom, following the sexual escapades of Valerie. A few years later the film's star, Danielle Ouimet, was arrested, not for baring all but for smuggling heroin into the U.S.*

A master of cinéma vérité, *Allan King first outraged censors with the sound track of* Warrendale, *his 1967 documentary about emotionally disturbed kids. Two years later the scissors were out again when he shot A Married Couple, a key-hole view of the turbulent prelude to an actual marriage breakup.*

CHAPTER THREE

The New Morality

I think you once agreed when I said that the state had no place in the bedrooms of the nation. I think we could say that the nation has no place in the bedrooms of the state ...

Pierre Trudeau in London, England, January 16, 1969

In 1960, a Montreal bookseller was convicted of peddling obscenity for selling the book *Lady Chatterley's Lover*, and when novelists Morley Callaghan and Hugh MacLennan defended it as a work of art, they were officially denounced by the Health League of Canada for having "contributed to the spread of adultery, prostitution and veneral disease in Canada." By 1969, the corner cigar store displayed a score of more magazines, mostly for men but some for women, that carried pictures and stories beyond Lady Chatterley's wildest imaginings.

When the decade was young, University of Western Ontario sociologist William Mann reported that there was no sexual revolution on campus, that only thirteen per cent of women students and thirty-five per cent of males had ever had sex. When the decade was old, an eighteen-year-old student from New Westminster, British Columbia, told a magazine writer: "Sex is so casual that a guy asks you to dinner and afterwards you go home, get undressed like old married people and, you know, just go to bed." She added a mild com-

plaint: "I'm not saying I'd like to be raped on the living room floor exactly, but I would like to sit around the sofa and neck a bit first."

If attitudes toward sex changed in the sixties, it was mainly because of the pill. In 1960, after eight years of experiments on animals and women in Puerto Rico, medical scientists pronounced the contraceptive pill safe for humans. At the time, there was hardly a hint of what the first foolproof and apparently harmless oral contraceptive would do to the world.

After the introduction of the pill, there was clear evidence that for all their publicly stated moral qualms about prescribing the pill to single women, doctors were doing precisely that. Responding to a survey, University of Toronto women students said two out of five doctors would prescribe the pill to the unmarried. Dr. M. M. Spivack said one-third of the five hundred to whom he prescirbed the pill were unmarried. "It's most unusual nowadays to see virgins over 18," he added.

At first, the pill simply represented freedom from unwanted pregnancy. Soon we were talking of "the permissive society" – permissive because sex only for the sake of pleasure was now possible. Most affected, of course, were younger women. In 1966, a University of Ottawa psychologist-counsellor said of them: "Our girls think that petting is dirty because it's teasing. They feel that if you're

Larry Kent's 1964 film Caressed *(later titled* Sweet Substitute) *dealt with a high school student's cope-and-grope loss of innocence. Much of the fine footage was left on the cutting-room floor before the film was allowed its premiere at the Montreal Film Festival.*

Midnight, Tab, True Secrets, Allo Police, Vedettes *and a dozen other scandal sheets all but covered up the news and women's magazines at this kiosk on Montreal's Peel Street.*

going to do that it's better to have intercourse, to go all the way."

While sociologists, doctors and psychologists seemed free to talk with candour about sex, journalists and writers sometimes found themselves "on the carpet" for saying the same thing. In the May 1963 issue of *Maclean's*, Pierre Berton – a writer well on his way to becoming a household name – labelled the use of sex in advertising "the great twentieth century hoax." He denounced a society that allowed its magazines and media to portray sex as the key to paradise and yet legally denied couples the pleasure until they were respectably married. The conflict between what young people were taught by advertising and what they were taught by the church caused "the sense of guilt, shame and sin which keeps young people in a state of constant emotional tension." He would, he wrote, prefer his own children to "indulge in some good, honest, satisfying sex than be condemned to a decade of whimpering frustration brought on by the appalling North American practice called petting."

There was a roar of outraged protest in newspapers and on the radio and television, and Berton's column ceased to appear in *Maclean's*. But clearly, sex was coming out of the closet, and the most convincing evidence of the "new morality" was seen on the newsstands, in places of entertainment, and in fashion.

a $1,000 centrefold

When nineteen-year-old Pamela Anne Gordon of Vancouver appeared as a *Playboy* magazine centrefold, she proudly announced she posed in the buff for the $1,000 fee, and "because I think it's a marvellous thing, not so much for myself but for Canada."

Canada got its first topless dancers at a bar called The Cat's Whiskers in Vancouver in August

1966. By the end of the decade most of the bigger Canadian cities had their own "sin strip" even if it was only half a block long. Dowdy, prudish old Toronto, which in 1960 even forbade movies and organized sports on Sundays, in 1969 boasted "adult" cinemas showing "soft-porn" movies on closed-circuit television; restaurants with half-naked waitresses, bars with bare-breasted go-go dancers and hole-in-the-wall bookstores where they did a roaring trade in vividly illustrated books with titles like *Lust Stop*, *Lust Lease* and *Call Boy*.

go-go girls

In 1967, *Star Weekly* writer Peter Sypnowich reported that go-go dancers, – young girls who stood on pedestals and sometimes even in cages, and twisted to the sound of rock music – were often the girl-next-door from suburbia, a college co-ed by day and a bar girl by night.

At a bar-cum-restaurant on Toronto's Yonge Street Strip, the luncheon special included the opportunity to daub paint on a naked girl who sat on a stool in the middle of the dance floor. A Vancouver businessmen's restaurant enlivened its lunches by staging strip shows by amateurs only. In Toronto's Yorkville there was a club called The Mynah Bird. At the door a lady with greying hair sat by the till, knitting, endlessly repeating the litany: "Topless bar straight through. Paint the nude on your right. Dirty movies upstairs on the left. That'll be two dollars cover charge please."

In 1964, Paris designers introduced the "see-through" dress. After selling almost two thousand of them, Chandler's on Toronto's Bloor Street decided it would do better if it sold flesh-coloured undies for the modest. Next came the totally topless swim suit, which sold better in Vancouver than elsewhere in Canada. Most were probably never seen outside fenced-in backyards, but one girl wore her topless suit on a Lake Ontario beach

Before bars went "topless," live burlesque houses like Toronto's Victory still packed them in, especially for "Amateur Night." Of course, the morality squad never missed a show.

Paperback Jungle

It wasn't because writers had gone sex-crazy that paperback book racks became jungles of soft-core erotica. After all, hardcover fiction still appeared with sedate jackets. Nor was sex much of a novelty as a merchandising gimmick – years before advertisers had discovered they could sell anything from hair colouring to Caribbean vacations with suggestive photos and copy. While the economics of scale kept Canadian publishers on the sidelines of the "racket," many U.S. mass-market houses adopted a "Sex Sells Everything" formula. So what if the "packaging" enticed some people to buy a book and others to flip pages for the steamy parts? The fine line between literature and a titillating read was academic anyway.

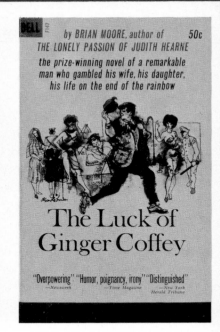

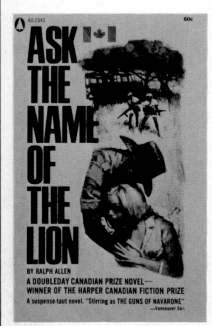

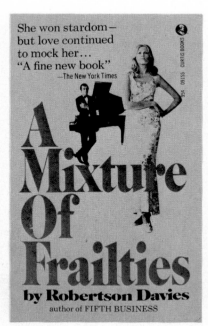

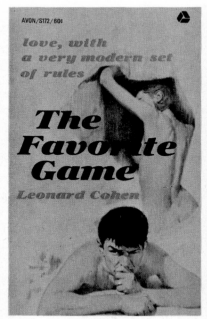

Some bookbuyers who had paid $4.95 or more for hardcover copies of these Canadian novels must have flinched when the under-a-buck editions appeared in stores. Hyped by copywriters as stories of "suspense, romance, sex, brutality and passion," mass-market paperbacks changed publishing into a "read it and throw it away" business. And if you didn't want to read the book, $1.50 would get you in to see the movie version of A Jest of God *or* The Luck of Ginger Coffey.

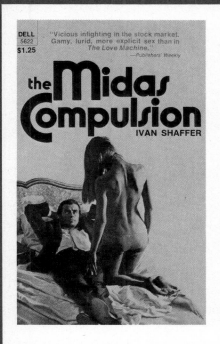

DELL 5622 $1.25

"Vicious infighting in the stock market. Gamy, lurid, more explicit sex than in *The Love Machine.*"
—Publishers' Weekly

the Midas Compulsion

IVAN SHAFFER

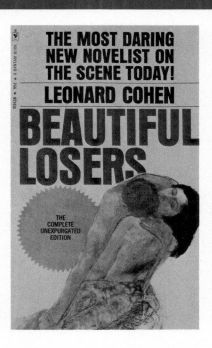

THE MOST DARING NEW NOVELIST ON THE SCENE TODAY!

LEONARD COHEN

BEAUTIFUL LOSERS

THE COMPLETE UNEXPURGATED EDITION

The outrageous new anti-establishment novel—"Saucy, dirty, abrasive, hilarious!"
—The New York Times

Cock-sure

by Mordecai Richler

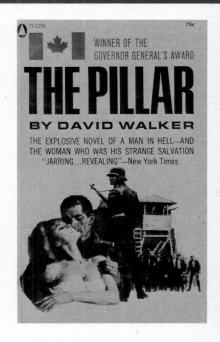

75-1256   75¢

WINNER OF THE GOVERNOR GENERAL'S AWARD

THE PILLAR

BY DAVID WALKER

THE EXPLOSIVE NOVEL OF A MAN IN HELL—AND THE WOMAN WHO WAS HIS STRANGE SALVATION
"JARRING...REVEALING"—New York Times

Golden Boy

Jackie Greenstein, golden boy of the street, was out for his biggest killing—with just one place to go for the edge he needed. Jackie knew, when he went to the man called Cort, he was putting his life in hock to The Family. Too late he learned that the Mafia also had a mortgage on his soul.

"Sex and the stockmarket . . . the story of Jackie Greenstein, who wheels and deals in stocks and women."
—Dayton News Tribune

"Taut play-by-play accounts of stock operations . . . tangled manipulations and financial intrigue . . . utterly fascinating"
—The New York Times

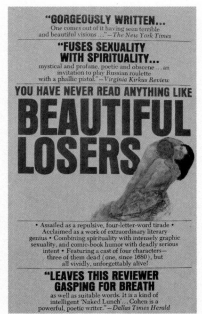

"GORGEOUSLY WRITTEN...
One comes out of it having seen terrible and beautiful visions . . ."—The New York Times

"FUSES SEXUALITY WITH SPIRITUALITY...
mystical and profane, poetic and obscene . . . an invitation to play Russian roulette with a phallic pistol."—Virginia Kirkus Review

YOU HAVE NEVER READ ANYTHING LIKE

BEAUTIFUL LOSERS

• Assailed as a repulsive, four-letter-word tirade •
Acclaimed as a work of extraordinary literary genius • Combining spirituality with intensely graphic sexuality, and comic-book humor with deadly serious intent • Featuring a cast of four characters—three of them dead (one, since 1680), but all vividly, unforgettably alive!

"LEAVES THIS REVIEWER GASPING FOR BREATH
as well as suitable words. It is a kind of intelligent 'Naked Lunch'...Cohen is a powerful, poetic writer."—Dallas Times Herald

Cock-sure

is "Shocking, disgusting, scatological, dirty, clever, near-pornographic, funny, embarrassing, nauseating, bewildering, cynical, uninhibited, unruly, unabashed and very interesting. I'm glad I read it!"
—San Francisco Chronicle

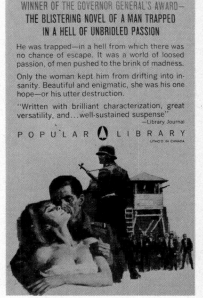

WINNER OF THE GOVERNOR GENERAL'S AWARD—
THE BLISTERING NOVEL OF A MAN TRAPPED IN A HELL OF UNBRIDLED PASSION

He was trapped—in a hell from which there was no chance of escape. It was a world of loosed passion, of men pushed to the brink of madness.

Only the woman kept him from drifting into insanity. Beautiful and enigmatic, she was his one hope—or his utter destruction.

"Written with brilliant characterization, great versatility, and...well-sustained suspense"
—Library Journal

POPULAR LIBRARY

Literary merits sometimes got second, third or no billing at all as writers and publishers dropped their euphemisms and readers came out of the closet. The natural relationships between men and women, in any combination or permutation, suddenly seemed worth writing and reading about. Oh, there were still a good many blushes and tsk-tsks, but no one was twisting anyone's arm to buy, read or browse through books like Beautiful Losers *and* Cocksure. *Right?*

"Protected by Canadian copyright," taboo to anyone under 21, stag films made money not only for "skin-flick" producers, distributors and models, but for the government as well. Ontario, notorious for its Blue Laws and bannings, got 3% of "the action" in provincial sales tax.

near Hamilton, and a local resident, Joseph Osborne reported her to the police. He had, he said, been observing the offensive sight of this topless sun-worshipper for ninety minutes (to give her a chance to cover herself decently), but since she failed to do so, he thought the police should prosecute. They didn't, though they could have under the Criminal Code.

anti-flesh blitz

In Quebec City in 1965, a municipal law forbidding women to display their thighs was still enforced, and in mid-summer, newly appointed police chief Gerard Girard sent fifty patrolmen to the old city for an eight day anti-flesh blitz. They handed out warnings that told women in shorts: "Cover your thighs or risk a find of $100 or three months in jail."

Police Chief Girard notwithstanding, skirts had inched upward throughout the decade, and Canadian women were clearly ready for the mini-skirt when it finally arrived from Britain in 1966. Some Canadian men were not, however. At the time, a promising young Toronto actor, invited eighteen-year-old Parisienne Dani Gruas to the premiere of one of English Canada's few feature films. Dani wore the latest Paris fashion, an evening suit in silver lame with a skirt four inches above the knee. When he saw her, the man gazed with mingled desire and dismay and said. "I can't take you dressed like that," and promptly walked out. Dani and two friends who had adopted the fashion drove to the premiere and picketed the performance brandishing signs that read "Square" and "Rat Fink."

By the end of the decade, fickle fashion had changed once again, and the new look was "unisex"–clothes designed to make men and women indistinguishable. If fashion reflects the attitudes of society, then the "unisex" statement was sexual equality, and by the late-1960s even advertisers were telling women, "You've come a long way, baby."

When the first grumblings of the "new feminists" were heard in the early sixties, they were either ignored or not noticed by mediamen. *Saturday Night* editor, Robert Fulford, suggested that the "women problem" was nothing more than a fad. *Maclean's* writer Christina Newman thought differently. In a 1962 article she attacked the women's pages of newspapers as "a collection of clichés and clap-trap, syndicated syrup and trumped-up trash, all of which presents a picture of women as an inferior sex living inferior lives."

Hundreds of other women agreed. In the mid-1960s, what had been a loose alliance of women's groups coalesced into the Committee for the Equality of Women, led by Mrs. Laura Sabia, a mother of four and a member of the St. Catharine's, Ontario, city council. She described women's plight this way:

We're still chained to the Biblical concept of women as virginal, submissive, seductive and totally left out of all decision making. It's a concentration camp of comfort.

Pressure from Mrs. Sabia's committee led Prime Minister Lester Pearson to set up a royal commission on the status of women in 1966, with journalist Anne Francis (she preferred to be called Mrs. John Bird) as its head.

status of women

When the commission opened hearings, witnesses told them horror story upon horror story. Women teachers still lost seniority when they left to have babies. The law still said a girl of twelve could marry if she was pregnant, but only if her father said so; the mother had no say in the matter. A commission survey showed that women consti-

"Hot" psychedelic Day-Glo colours became the rage in fashion around 1968. As the hemlines of mini-skirts and dresses rose to mid-thigh, the waistline disappeared, and bell-bottomed "hip-hugger" pants and "rib-tickler" blouses made the bare midriff the focus of erotic attention.

While the Royal Commission on the Status of Women was studying sex-stereotyping in school books and job want-ads, angry feminists were beginning to muster enough clout to force ad agencies to think twice before running blatantly sexist advertisements, such as the one above.

tuted more than half the population, – and had less than one per cent of the top decision-making jobs in business, industry or government. Only nine per cent of Canada's professionals were women – only seven per cent of doctors, three per cent of lawyers, one per cent of engineers. There were almost no day-care facilities where a child could be left while the mother worked, and so women abandoned by husbands were forced to stay home, barely existing on welfare handouts. A wife who worked was penalized by the income tax department. Even if doctors decided a woman should have an abortion to save her life, they were obliged to get the husband's permission before performing the operation. Said Anne Francis: "The attitudes of some Canadian men are ghastly – Victorian and antiquated."

Mexican divorce mill

Canada's archaic divorce laws remained unchanged for most of the decade. Adultry had been the only legal ground for divorce in eight provinces. There was no divorce at all in Quebec and Newfoundland; to end a marriage, residents had to ask the House of Commons to pass a private act of parliament. All this produced a curious moral ambiguity. Men and women who wanted to remarry but were reluctant to "live in sin" trekked south to Mexico to get a divorce that wasn't recognized in Canada, and then went to one of the American states where laws were less rigid – Nevada, for instance – to re-marry and returned to Canada as Mr. and Mrs., despite the fact that neither the divorce nor the subsequent second marriage was legally valid in Canada. A multi-million-dollar Mexican divorce mill flourished in Canada in the late 1960s. Living together after a Mexican divorce was no less sinful, but by spending so much to be as legal as possible, consciences were eased.

In 1969, the divorce laws were changed to include the grounds of cruelty, desertion and simple "marital breakdown." More important, judges could grant a divorce without deciding who was the "guilty" party. It meant the law no longer presumed that marriage was a lifelong undertaking, and in this way the state finally caught up with the Anglican and United churches which earlier in the decade had stopped insisting " . . . 'til death do us part" be included in the wedding service.

women's liberation

At about the same time, Section 208 of the Criminal Code, which outlawed abortions except to save the woman's life, was changed. The new law permitted abortions to preserve the life *and* *health* of a woman. Hospitals set up abortion committees of doctors who generally felt free to perform an abortion if an unwanted pregnancy was damaging to mental health. Suddenly legal abortions were available in Canada.

The women's liberation movement also turned its attention to the problem of underwear, in its early lunacy condemning as symbols of male suppression. In less moderate and reasonable places feminists actually burned their bras in public. In Canada some just quit wearing them.

It was at about this time that humorist Robert Thomas Allen's daughter explained to him that holding the door for a woman was evidence that a man didn't acknowledge the total equality of the opposite sex. And Vancouver-born anthropologist Dr. Lionel Tiger said publicly that a general revolt by women was imminent and "will make the black problem in the United States look comparatively easy to solve."

Before the amendment of the Criminal Code legalized therapeutic abortions in 1968, some 100,000 women each year were forced to seek out shady "doctors" or have the operation performed abroad. Hailed by some as a landmark in women's rights, others called the Bill a "mandate for murder."

artscanada

The revolution in Canadian art in the '60s was not the slavish shift from one imported style to another – from Abstract Impressionism to American Pop, Op, Hard-Edge or Realism – but the emergence of independent, often nationalistic, artists who saw imitation as a dead-end. If the works of Bloore or Bush, Chambers or Molinari, Pratt, Tousignant or Town appeared in galleries, it was not because of some foreign critic's seal of approval.

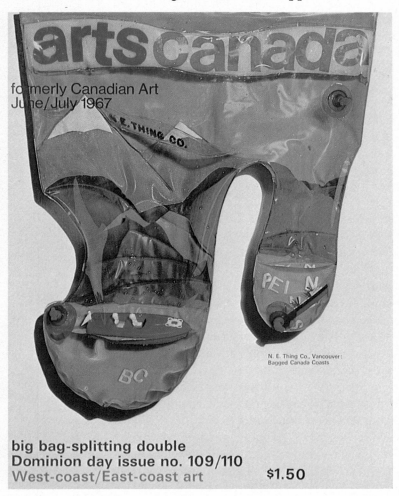

artscanada

formerly
Canadian Art
January 1967
issue no.104
75¢

**Salute to Centennial:
your guide
to the arts in '67 celebrations**

Greg Curnoe. For Ben Bella

artscanada

formerly Canadian Art
June/July 1967

N.E. THING CO.

N. E. Thing Co., Vancouver:
Bagged Canada Coasts

**big bag-splitting double
Dominion day issue no. 109/110
West-coast/East-coast art** $1.50

Greg Curnoe's For Ben Bella – *satirizing Mackenzie King, the liberal who "sold us to the U.S.A." (according to the painting) – spelled-out* artscanada *magazine's new nationalistic policy for Centennial year.*

Vancouver's Iain Baxter dubbed plastic "the pottery of today" and set up the pseudo-serious N.E. Thing Company as the artistic manufactory of outrageous polyethylene creations, such as Bagged Canada Coasts.

During Michael Snow's five-year "affair" with his "Walking Woman" he reworked this simple image in a hundred variations: in painting (such as Mixed Feelings, *above), sculpture, film and even a rubber stamp.*

A 1920s photograph of two lynched Blacks (published in U.B.C.'s Ubyssey) *prompted Vancouver's Claude Breeze to paint* Sunday Afternoon: From an Old American Photograph – *one of his many stark and brutal social comments.*

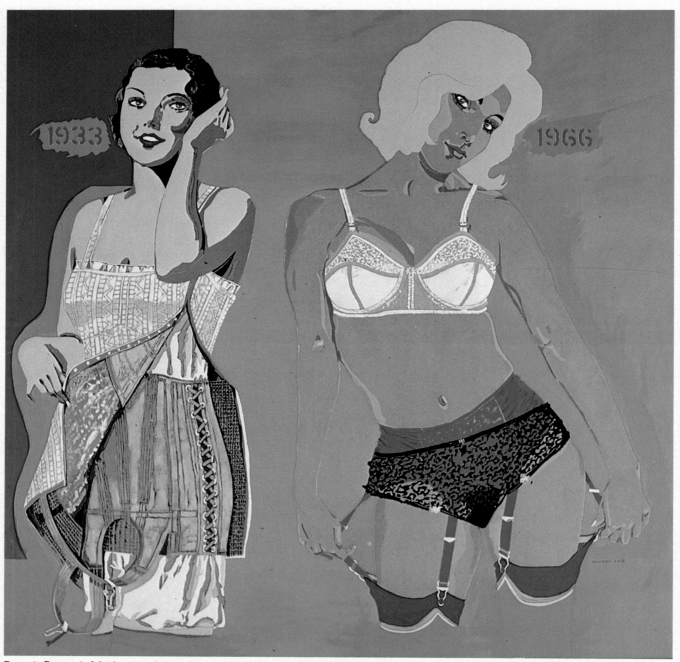

Dennis Burton's Mothers and Daughters *(1966) was one of his first* post-abstract "Garterbeltmania" *works – an obsession he traced back to boyhood days in Lethbridge, Alberta, his father's art scrapbook, underwear ads, comics and pulp magazines.*

CHAPTER FOUR

Pop Arts

I am simply trying to make art more accessible to everyone.

Joyce Wieland, 1967

The exhibition of seventeen works by the hitherto unknown Saskatchewan sculptor Wyn Hedore was the most successful in the seven-year history of Regina's Norman Mackenzie Art Gallery. The catalogue, listing prices up to $250, described the works as "a fantastic series of almost speaking images." Some visitors were outraged but generally the local culturati murmured approvingly, some saying the show was proof that Regina – nay, Canada even – had caught up with the rest of the world, and that the works were the equal of anything you could find in New York.

Two drew special comment – *The Huckster*, which resembled an automobile crankshaft upended on a Chevrolet nameplate; and a work called simply *Pail*, described in the catalogue as "a straightforward, realistic study of concentration on a simple and basic form." *Pail* was exhibited on a pedestal of grey stone, cunningly lit from above. The price was $175.

It was October 1960, and it hadn't been a good year for wheat, but even so there were potential buyers. When someone offered to buy *Pail* a week after the exhibition opened, gallery director Ronald Bloore was forced to own up: he and two painter friends had fashioned the "sculptures" from bits and pieces scrounged from the provincial government transport garage. The work *Huckster* didn't just resemble an upended crankshaft; it *was* one. And *Pail* was just that – a pail which, if it hadn't been flattened by a passing car, would have sold for $2.92 at the local hardware store.

Bloore, himself a well-known painter, had set out "to jolt Reginans into developing their own notions of art instead of slavishly adopting the definitions of artists and critics of other places, New York mostly."

Canadian artists – from writers to puppeteers – had traditionally gone to Paris, London and New York to earn recognition. Early in the 1960s, Canada lost of group of brilliant film makers to Hollywood, and one of them, Arthur Hiller, said that in Britain and the United States "recognition of creativity comes easier." What was perhaps the most important musical of the decade, *Hair*, had a score written by Montrealer Galt MacDermot, who was a hero on Broadway and the former director of the Westmount Baptist Church choir in Montreal.

Painter Frederick Varley, one of the original Group of Seven, *proved* you couldn't be an artist very comfortably in Canada: he never worked outside the country. It wasn't until 1960, when he was eighty, that he earned enough from painting to make an income tax return necessary. Sculptor Gerald Gladstone, whose work was lauded in Britain and New York (the New York *Herald-Tribune*

Gratien Gélinas' compelling drama, Hier les Enfants Dansaient, *about a family divided over separatism, saw its English premiere at the 1967 Charlottetown Festival, with the playwright and his two sons in the lead roles. The production was Gélinas' second collaboration with director-translator Mavor Moore – the dean of English Canadian theatre.*

SHAW
FESTIVAL
1968

NIAGARA-ON-THE-LAKE
CANADA

When the Shaw Festival opened its first season in 1962 in the old, renovated Court House in sleepy Niagara-on-the-Lake, critics and cynics figured the event would survive a couple of years at best. (A decade before some had said the same about Stratford's Shakespeare Festival.) By 1970, the 200-year-old town was being restored to its colonial charm, a magnificent new theatre was on the drawing boards, and the company, under directors Andrew Allan, Barry Morse and Paxton Whitehead, had become a showcase of Canadian acting talent.

described his sculptures as "infernal machines of beauty and power"), was condemned by Canadian critics for self-promotion. Said Gladstone: "I worked in advertising for ten years and I know that in this country people don't admire talent; they admire popularity. So I'm seeking publicity to become popular."

cultural identity

All this, however, was a more or less familiar story. What was new, and encouraging, was that at the start of the 1960s there was a groundswell of resentment of American domination of Canadian culture. By the end of the decade it had become such a strong wave of anti-Americanism that one critic claimed it was actually healthy. University of Toronto historian Frank Underhill argued in 1961, that no race had ever "built up a good, lively nationalist spirit without an enemy whom it could hate heartily."

Underhill was, of course, talking about the attitude of English Canada toward the United States. However, he might just as well have been discussing the attitude of French Canada toward English Canada and the U.S. By the end of the 1960s, we had established a healthy and most distinctive "Canadian" culture. When it came to cultural identity, Quebec was there ahead of English Canada in every field – visual arts, theatre, film, music, literature and, above all, television.

No two men symbolized the difference in the cultural development of "deux nations" more than Gratien Gélinas and Mavor Moore. Both were actor-playwrights of considerable talent, the first well known in Quebec, the latter in English Canada. Gélinas felt free to write of the social and political realities of his own society. His 1966 *Hier Les Enfants Dansaient* (*Yesterday The Children Were Dancing*) was about a generation then more interested in separatism and learning to make bombs

than in dancing. Moore, no less a talent, functioned in a society that cared little for its own affairs but was mesmerized by the activities of the United States and Britain. Moore's significant contributions to the awakening theatre of English Canada were a score of productions of Canadian plays, among them the historical opera *Louis Riel*.

folksingers and chansonniers

Down the street from the theatre in the concert halls, coffee houses, bistros and clubs, the music and lyrics of Canadian singers and groups became worth listening to. Ian Tyson and Sylvia Fricker topped folk charts with songs like "Four Strong Winds"; Gordon Lightfoot with "The Canadian Railway Trilogy" and "Early Morning Rain"; Joni Mitchell with "Both Sides Now"; Leonard Cohen with "Suzanne"; Buffy Sainte-Marie with "Now That The Buffalo's Gone."

In Quebec the young gathered in smoky cafés to hear the *chansonniers* sing of tradition and separatism. This lyric by Gilles Vigneault was typical:

I've sold my fir tree for a street lamp
The street lamp dims the dawn;
I've sold the salmon and even the river
To some English millionaires.
And I've learned by selling so much
That without my birthright I'm a servant again.

But all was not nationalism even in Quebec. Bands, known as "ye ye groups," played the same ear-shattering rock 'n' roll as the Beatles. One group, *Les Classels*, dressed in white top hats, white tail suits, played white instruments, wore white wigs, drove around in white limousines – and needed police protection because of over-enthusiastic fans. When *Les Classels* and a half dozen other pop music groups staged a concert in November 1964, more than 14,000 teenagers packed the Quebec Coliseum to shout, scream and some-

50

Blind-Man's-Buff

Toronto Telegram *cartoonist Al Beaton (one of the great editorial wits of the decade) summed up the "Canadian Culture Debate" in this one brilliant parable. After Centennial, only the odd academic still psycho-analyzed the nation's "inferiority complex"; most artists by then saw the notion as a load of elephant manure.*

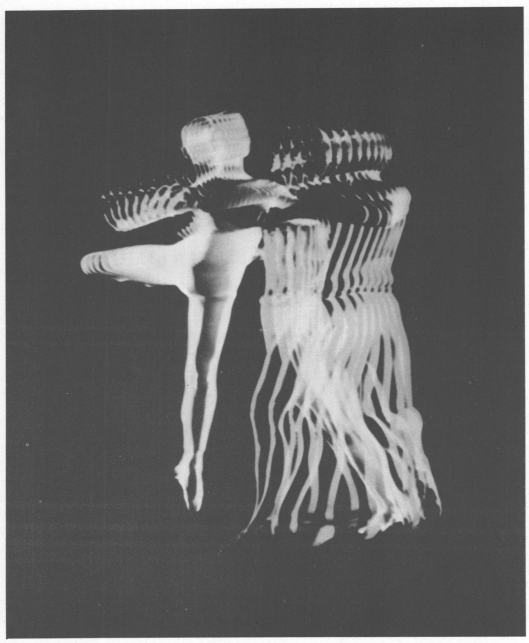

Over 100 international awards (including an Oscar in '52 for Neighbors) *have guaranteed* NFB *film-maker Norman McLaren a front-row-centre seat in the movie "hall of fame." The "still" above is from* Pas de Deux *(an Academy Award nominee in '67), a pioneer in film technique.*

times even listen. A similar concert by local bands in Toronto the same year drew an audience of fewer than a thousand. In English Canada the kids worshipped the groups imported from Britain and the United States.

But it was in television that French Canadians most obviously demonstrated the truth of Frank Underhill's "healthy hate" contention. At its birth in the fifties, the CBC French language network could not import shows from France because television had not yet taken root in that country. French Canada had to produce its own. By 1960, Montreal was the largest French language television production centre in the world.

As the Fowler Royal Commission on Canadian Broadcasting subsequently pointed out, more than three-quarters of the programmes on English-Canadian television were either American or British imports. And at that, Commissioner Fowler found them "stupefyingly mediocre." While television in French Canada spent *millions* creating its own superstars, Fowler found that in 1965, the average private English-Canadian station spent a paltry $110 a day employing Canadian performers, writers and directors.

The cultural differences between French and English Canada were underlined by the style as well as the number of homemade shows. One of English Canada's most popular programmes during the 1960s was the American-made "Candid Camera" which spied on people in allegedly amusing situations. English Canada laughed at Americans arguing with San Francisco store clerks, harassing Miami bus drivers and confronting talking mail boxes in New York. When Quebec producers stole the candid camera idea, their first show used infra-red film to catch unsuspecting Montrealers in the back rows of a movie house.

Because the shows French Canadians and English Canadians watched were so different, television nourished separatism without even trying. In mid-decade, there was no one in English Canada who had not heard of the CBC Sunday night show "This Hour Has Seven Days"—and very few in French Canada who had. "Seven Days" was an unlikely news and public affairs programme, a marriage of show business and journalism that was irreverent, outrageous, sometimes vulgar and full of vitality. Unlike most public affairs television, it didn't report things happening—it made them happen. The show made news itself as often as it reported it. Once it staged a sketch showing the Pope being asked to referee a baseball game, a feature which drew more calls and letters of outrage than anything in previous CBC history. Once it invited leaders of the Ku Klux Klan to don robes and explain that they weren't really racists, then confronted them with a Black interviewer.

With such tactics—and despite its peak audience of three million—"Seven Days" became an embarrassment to the management of the CBC, who cancelled the show in April 1966. The cancellation drew more calls of protest (7,400) than even the Pope sketch. As a result, Parliament publicly debated the role of the CBC, and thirty of the nation's academics, journalists and politicians protested that the killing of "Seven Days" made them fear the CBC was becoming "an organization shorn of its proper function (of stimulating debate) by the dead hand of conformity."

Even though the state-owned, tax-subsidized television network wasn't pivotal in developing an English Canadian popular culture during the sixties, government money was very visible in other areas, most notably the building of theatres, art galleries, and museums.

It began in the west in the late 1950s and early 1960s with the Queen Elizabeth Theatre in Vancouver and the Jubilee Auditoriums in Edmonton and Calgary. Thereafter the building of "cultural centres," almost all of them paid for by federal and/or provincial and municipal tax money, em-

Toronto reviewers who panned Don Owen's Nobody Waved Goodbye *after its Canadian premiere in 1964 had to eat crow when, months later, New York's top critics hailed the film (starring Peter Kastner and Julie Biggs, above) as a sensitive and honest portrayal of troubled youth.*

London, Ontario artist Jack Chambers, here at work on 401 Towards London, #1, *was among the first painters to resurrect realism (he called it "perceptualism"). Making no apology for his everyday subject matter, he said, "I am not interested in art, I am interested in life."*

ployed a young army of architects and builders throughout the decade. More than 2,500 theatres, art galleries, museums and zoos were built in Canada as Centennial projects, ranging from halls in prairie villages and remote mining towns to the $46-million, 2,300-seat National Arts Centre in Ottawa which opened in 1969.

But for all the splendour of the new surroundings, the culture was still mostly imported. When the Neptune Theatre opened in Halifax in 1963 – an event that critics hailed as evidence of "a new era in Canadian culture" – there were four plays in its repertory, two by American playwrights, one by George Bernard Shaw and one a translation from the French.

When something called "the Canadian Identity" emerged toward the end of the decade, it did so most apparently in literature. Again, French Canada had led the way. In the early 1960s the University of Birmingham in Britain was prompted to set up a special course to study French-Canadian literature.

nothing north of the 48th parallel

At the beginning of the decade most English Canadians were reading books imported from the United States. In Montreal in the opening years of the 1960s the English language schools were using a grade four reader that gave lessons on how to pledge allegiance to the Stars and Stripes. In British Columbia schools, one book taught time zones differences with a map of the United States, and on the prairies a textbook map of the "national forests" showed nothing north of the 48th parallel. One textbook, allegedly "revised" for Canadian use, talked of the American Civil War as "our own war." Our mounting nationalism changed that. Of 1,800 new titles published in Canada between 1960 and 1966, almost 1,600 were textbooks and reference books. Only 200 were general interest books

54

– books of reportage or opinion, novels or volumes of poetry. The 1967 Centennial inspired writers and publishers to produce a stream of books that celebrated Canada and the Canadian experience.

guerillas of the new writing

Four new small publishing houses opened with the aim of publishing young writers who deserved to be heard but were ignored by apprehensive "established" publishers. A *Maclean's* magazine reporter visited the House of Anansi a year after it was established and, awestruck, reported:

The difficulty of access – a handwritten sign on the house's locked front door directs you around the corner into a side street, down the second driveway on the right, through a back garden gate, down the wooden steps, past the furnace room and the cardboard boxes stacked with George Grant's Technology and Empire *– and the constant comings and goings of serious young people give it something of the feeling of a bunker in the siege of Stalingrad. Here guerillas of the new writing plot daring forays; here at dawn a young novelist rolls up from his sleeping bag upon the concrete floor of the furnace room and shouts that at last he understands his central character. Here is the future.*

It was in part the books produced by these and other "little" publishing houses that later led Northrop Frye, Canada's best known critic, to write of "the colossal verbal explosion that has taken place in Canada since 1960." Between 1817 and 1960, fewer than 600 biographies of Canadians were published; as many again were published during the 1960s. In the same decade more than 1,000 volumes of poetry were published by more than 500 poets.

Frye made his comments in Volume III of the *Literary History of Canada*. The first two volumes covered everything published between the arrival of Jacques Cartier and 1960. Volume III was devoted almost entirely to books published in the 1960s. The more significant of those books were by writers whose names had been familiar in the two previous decades. They included Morley Callaghan, Hugh MacLennan, Mordecai Richler, Thomas Raddall, Brian Moore and Robertson Davies. However in the renaissance in Canadian literature during the 1960s, the new names of significance were those of women. Margaret Laurence, Marian Engel, Alice Munro and Margaret Atwood all published their first fiction during the decade.

And in his review of the 1960's Frye suggested that by the end of the decade anti-Americanism would no longer be necessary to Canada, that the United States' empire was in a decline, and that as a result Americans, newly aware that growth couldn't go on forever, were actually becoming more like Canadians. He added: "Meanwhile, Canada, traditionally so diffident, introverted, past and future fixated, incoherent, inarticulate, proceeding by hunch and feeling, seems to be taking on, at least culturally, an inner composure and integration of outlook, even some buoyancy and confidence."

Well, by 1969 that may have been true of literature. But Ronald Bloore, who began the 1960s by staging a spectacular hoax at the Regina art gallery, was by no means convinced. Wyn Hedore was a name manufactured from Bloore's own name and that of his partners in the hoax. In 1968, the highly respectable Canadian Paperback Library published Volume II of *A Dictionary of Canadian Artists*. On page 414 was the entry: "HEDORE, Wyn: A Saskatchewan artist who exhibited his three-dimensional constructions [at the] Norman Mackenzie Gallery in Regina in the fall of 1960."

Until the opening of the National Arts Centre in May 1969, jokesters called Ottawa "the only cemetery in Canada with stoplights." Gone were the days. The NAC *Orchestra, under the baton of maestro Mario Bernardi (born in Kirkland Lake, Ontario), packed the concert hall with its first season's series. Monique Leyrac was "*SOLD OUT*" an hour after tickets went on sale. And visiting repertory companies from across the country filled the Studio Theatre night after night. Despite a few hitches (the Centre's own drama company fell apart in mid-season; the parking garage was a hopeless labyrinth), it wasn't a bad beginning for the multi-million-dollar complex regarded by some as the Liberals' latest "white elephant."*

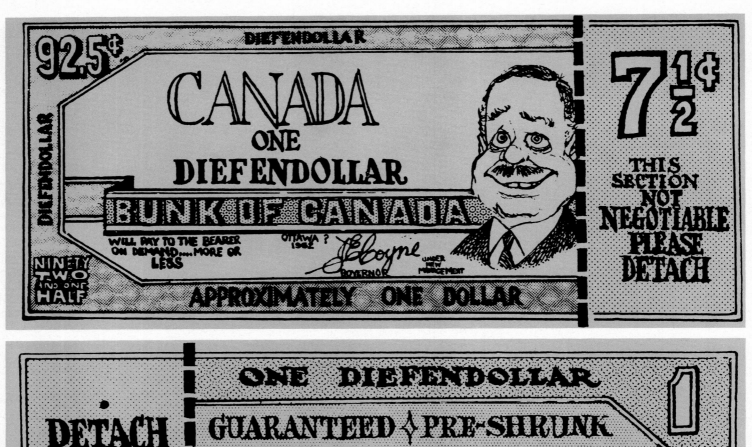

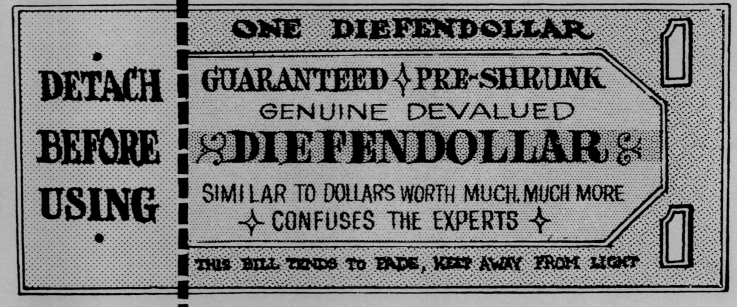

The "Diefenbuck" — "similar to dollars worth much, much more" — was an ingenious piece of Liberal propaganda in the '62 election campaign. Dief's finance minister Donald Fleming (who pegged the dollar at 92.5¢ U.S.) gives the gag-currency some "face-value."

CHAPTER FIVE

Easy Money

Money: The Poor Man's Credit Card.

Marshall McLuhan, *Understanding Media*, 1964

What's worth more than money? In the middle of the sixties, the answer to that question would have been gold. By the end of the decade the answer was plastic.

But first things first. Traditionally, our dimes, quarters and half-dollars were made of eighty per cent silver, and so long as the world market price of silver stayed around $1.70 an ounce, they were *worth* ten, twenty-five and fifty cents. But in 1966 silver broke that value barrier, and suddenly our coins were too valuable to spend. The following year, the Royal Mint in Ottawa cut the silver content of 1967 Centennial coins to fifty per cent, so that coins then contained their face value in silver. A similar situation existed in the United States, and the Washington mint cut the silver content of American coins. Still in circulation, however, were billions of dollars worth of silver-heavy coins, all worth more on the silver market than in the supermarket.

It was illegal to damage or deface the coinage in either Canada or the United States, but Canadian coins could quite legally be melted down in the United States for their silver content, and vice versa. Neither government approved of too much coinage being shipped across its borders, largely because it meant a shortage of small change in stores. So millions of coins from both countries passed back and forth across the international border in fast power boats crossing the Great Lakes by night; in fishing boats and pleasure yachts on both east and west coasts; in private planes allegedly on pleasure trips; in the trunks of cars packed with vacationers; in falsely-labelled packing cases in rail box-cars. Coin merchants offering new-coins-for-old set up shop in the border towns and in all of Canada's bigger cities.

Bus drivers, store clerks, bank tellers, telephone company coin collectors ... anyone with access to coins in quantity sometimes made astonishing profits. They collected pre-1967 coins, sold them at twenty per cent profit (at the top of the market, a quarter was worth thirty cents), and took payment in new coins or paper money. Coin merchants sold the coins in bulk to bullion dealers across the border. One Vancouver man claimed to have financed his Hawaiian honeymoon this way. A Quebec City clerk who dealt with parking meter takings boasted that in three hectic months he made enough to buy a new car.

Then, in 1968, it happened all over again. The market price of silver went up again, and this time both Ottawa and Washington began making coins that contained no silver at all. These new quarters were worth barely five cents.

If money wasn't worth its weight in silver, gold

Mounting trade deficits during the "Diefenbaker Recession" of the late-'50s and early-'60s sparked "Buy Canadian" campaigns, particularly in the large manufacturing centres of Ontario's "Golden Horseshoe."

The flip-side of the PC's "100% Stable Canadian Dollar" (right): debunking "The Big Liberal Lie."

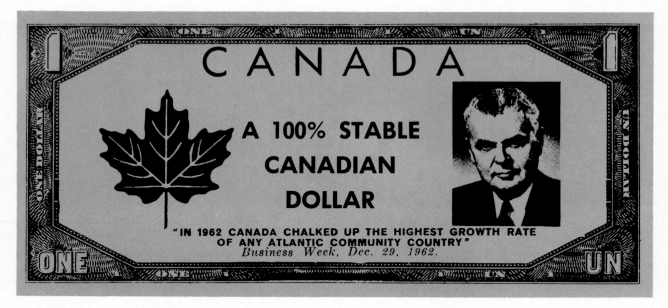

The Conservatives' 1963 campaign retort to the "Diefenbuck" (page 56) was this "100% Stable Canadian Dollar" and its attached list of devaluation dividends: increases in production, personal income, employment, exports and profits.

wasn't pulling its weight either. Canada had been a major world gold producer since the turn of the century. By 1966, however, more than thirty of the rich Timmins mines had closed because it cost more to dig the gold than it was worth. The San Antonio mine in Bissett, across the border in Manitoba, would have lost money had it paid miners more than $1.92 an hour, but by 1966, the minimum wage in a *copper* mine was $2.92 an hour.

By the time all this happened, however, gold and silver had precious little to do with whether we lived like paupers or kings. What really mattered was credit. Hardly anyone actually went out and spent real money any more; we spent the future. Nor did we just buy things like houses and cars and furniture. We went into debt for such things as dishwashers, washing machines, microwave ovens, refrigerator-freezers, electric can openers, coffee grinders, and other appliances that did just about everything that was once regarded

as household drudgery. Convenience cost money, and we paid with tomorrow. By the end of the decade, we were buying much of our lifestyle on credit – airline tickets and hotel rooms and package holidays that included both.

We did it mostly with pieces of plastic – the credit cards issued by twenty-one nation-wide organizations ranging from American Express through various gas companies, to the giant store chains like Eaton's, Simpson's, Woodward's, and The Bay. In 1968, four Canadian chartered banks launched Chargex. By 1969, the twenty-one national credit companies had issued at least seventeen million plastic passports to consumers. No one was sure whether it meant that Canadians suddenly had more faith in tomorrow than ever before, or whether we decided collectively that tomorrow might never come, so we might as well mortgage it to the hilt. Whatever the explanation, in 1960 the total credit debt in Canada amounted

Britain's dickering to join the Common Market revived the old debate over Canada's economic union with the U.S. *Should it happen,* Maclean's *proposed this design for the currency. (Note the beaver under the American eagle's wing.)*

to only $223 per person. By 1969 it was $515.

For all the money madness, it was not a decade plagued by inflation. Nor was it a decade in which we actually earned the improvement in our standard of living. We paid for it largely by selling Canadian resources and industry to foreigners, mostly Americans. In 1969, that realization came as a shock, but it shouldn't have: wise men warned us when the decade began, but they were either vilified or ignored.

James Coyne, then governor of the Bank of Canada, was one such soothsayer. He argued that since World War II, Canadians had largely been living off the proceeds of selling resources and industries to foreigners. Canadians, he said, were like a family that kept itself alive by selling its furniture, and even the house itself. Coyne advocated "tight money" – that is, belt-tightening restrictions on credit buying – and regulations to slow the rate at which foreign money was buying Canadian re-

sources, industry and real estate. Since that meant Canadians wouldn't be able to live as well as the Americans, it was not a policy that appealed either to the people or to politicians who needed votes. John Diefenbaker, then prime minister, forced out Coyne in 1961, and Canadians continued to enjoy the second-highest standard of living in the world.

Others who echoed Coyne were ignored. And by 1969, we had learned to live with the fact that a large slice of our national economy was owned by foreigners. Indeed, by that time we were welcoming deputations from a new industrial giant, Japan, which wanted to buy British Columbia resources, mostly wood and coal. Japanese money was involved elsewhere, and provided the classic example of the Canadian dilemma at Bathurst, New Brunswick. There in 1962 a new copper mine opened, providing needed jobs. Barely a hundred miles away in the Gaspé was a copper smelter working below capacity for lack of ore to process.

Not all the protesters of the '60s were long-haired hippy radicals. In fact, some, like Walter Gordon, wore three-piece, pin-striped suits and were respected leaders of the business and financial community. Shocked by the statistics unveiled by the 1955 commission he headed on Canada's Economic Prospects, as Liberal minister of finance in '63, he proposed stringent measures in his budget to control the expansion of foreign investment and control. Scorned by some MPs in his party and vilified by corporation heads, his avant-garde programme to "buy back Canada" – outlined in his book A Choice for Canada *(1965) – became the* raison d'être *for the Canada Development Corporation, the Foreign Investment Review Agency, and the Committee for an Independent Canada.*

Grinning Toronto Stock Exchange workers sweep up the paper blizzard after Texas Gulf Sulphur's April 16, 1964 announcement of huge ore finds near Timmins, Ontario, sparked frantic trading.

But ore from the Bathurst mine was shipped to a smelter in Japan.

Coyne's economic recipe was indigestible partly because he first offered it in 1960, when economists said Canada was midway through a mini-depression, and no one wanted to hear more bad news. Unemployment was high and money already tight.

Reassurance came from D. R. Buglass, advertising manager of Armstrong Cork of Canada, a flooring manufacturer, who informed us in 1960: "In the Depression the most common floor covering colour was red, to cheer people up I guess. Now all the leading floor coverings are neutral in colour. People don't need cheering up today."

spending spree

The Diefenbaker recession seemed merely a punctuation mark between the fabulous fifties and the soaring sixties. In 1962, we even went on an historic spending spree. Trade minister George Hees said that trying to meet consumer demand was "like trying to fill a bathtub with the plug left out."

Trouble was, most of the manufactured goods we bought had to be imported. We couldn't pay for them with exports, so Britain, the United States and the International Monetary Fund had to bail us out to prevent national bankruptcy, while the government introduced some austerity plans.

But the boom-to-bust-and-back-again pendulum was on an upswing for most of the rest of the decade, and by 1965, the Gross National Product – the total value of goods and services produced throughout the nation – had zoomed up to pass the $50 billion a year mark, five years ahead of all predictions. That year British Columbia's average industrial wage topped the magic $100-a-week mark. We also boasted more strikes than almost any other nation. In June 1965, there were eighty-five of them were under way.

According to some economists, strikes were most common when workers were wealthy and the future rosey. A common strike issue was that Canadians wanted to be paid as much as Americans, and in fact in mid-decade, the rate of Canadian wage increases was almost twice as high as the rate in the United States. By the 1960s, the unions were mostly Canadian branches of American unions—and many of the corporations they had to deal with were, in fact, subsidiaries of American parent companies.

bonanza

Meanwhile, the Canadian north continued to open up: at times it seemed that every month there was a new mineral or oil or gas discovery that merited headlines like "biggest" or "bonanza." American ownership grew, because it was usually American money that made the discoveries, or did the development work. In 1960, after a decade of negotiations, Canada and the United States finally agreed to a $3 billion project to build hydroelectric dams along British Columbia's Columbia River. Andrew McNaughton was head of the Canadian negotiating team, and when it ended he said of the deal: "The Canadians were a house divided, unskilled and uninformed, and they opened a situation for the Americans to exploit and were skinned alive."

But in the short run, when any new natural resource development or mining discovery was made, Canadians made fortunes too. A few days before Easter in 1964, geologist Kenneth Dark, an employee of the Texas Gulf Sulphur Company, stumbled out of the muskeg near Timmins, Ontario, and privately told his boss by phone that the company had struck it rich with one of the biggest copper finds in history. Prospectors promptly poured into the area from around the world in the

Pas de question.

Voici la carte de chèques garantis de la Banque de Nouvelle-Écosse.

À quoi sert cette carte?

Elle vous permet de payer par chèque là où on ne vous connaît pas. Elle vous permet également d'encaisser un chèque sans difficulté ni retard.

Qu'est-ce donc que cette carte?

En premier lieu, elle porte votre photographie. Cette photo est en couleur; elle vous identifie sans risque d'erreur.

En second lieu, elle établit sans le moindre doute que la Banque de Nouvelle-Écosse garantit le paiement de vos chèques, en tout lieu et en tout temps.

Évidemment, c'est votre photographie qui fait foi de tout. La carte de chèques garantis de la Banque de Nouvelle-Écosse vous identifie sur-le-champ; on peut donc accepter vos chèques en toute confiance.

La carte de chèques garantis possède un autre atout. S'il vous arrive de faire un chèque dont le montant dépasse ce que vous avez en banque, cette carte agit automatiquement comme une carte de crédit.

Que coûte-t-elle? À vous, deux dollars seulement. Et rien du tout aux personnes qui acceptent vos chèques.

Venez à la Banque de Nouvelle-Écosse. Nous prendrons votre photographie avec notre appareil-couleur exclusif.

Dès que vous aurez reçu votre carte, gardez-la toujours sur vous. Présentez-la chaque fois que vous faites un chèque: au magasin, au restaurant, partout.

Pas de retard, pas de problème, pas de question.

Lisez la garantie au verso de la carte.

La Banque de Nouvelle-Écosse garantit vos chèques. En tout lieu.

Châtelaine • octobre 1968

In 1968, the Bank of Nova Scotia issued what was, in effect, the first Canadian bank credit card. If Ann Edwards' face looks familiar, you saw her in the movie, A Married Couple *(page 36).*

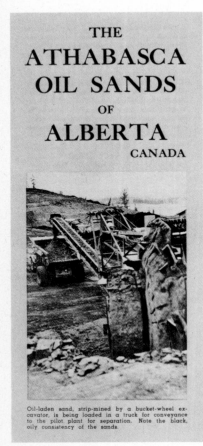

THE ATHABASCA OIL SANDS OF ALBERTA CANADA

Oil-laden sand, strip-mined by a bucket-wheel excavator, is being loaded in a truck for conveyance to the pilot plant for separation. Note the black, oily consistency of the sands.

Oil was still relatively cheap and supplies assumedly limitless when the Alberta government licensed the Sun Oil Company to begin work on its $300 million Great Canadian Oil Sands plant at Fort McMurray in 1964. Regarded by other firms as a precarious, long-range investment, Sunoco engineers kept in mind the estimated 300-billion-barrel reserve saturating the tar sands (over half the world's total supply), and by 1970 were producing about 45,000 barrels of oil per day.

biggest demonstration of money hunger since the Klondike gold rush. Shares in companies that were nothing more than names on paper went for pennies one day on the Toronto, Montreal and Vancouver Stock Exchanges, and for dollars the next.

Windfall Oils and Mines Limited was one such company. Before the strike, "Windfall" shares sold for 56¢ apiece on the Toronto Stock Exchange. After the "discovery," a whisper went around the speculators' haunts: "Windfall has found ore, too." The company issued no denials, and shares went to $5.60 apiece. Windfall president George MacMillan and his wife, Viola, bought and sold stock in their own company, and the judge that later convicted them both for illegal practices was told they made $1,455,928 profit in eleven days.

"stockateers"

The MacMillans were caught, but scores who played similar dizzy games with resource industry stocks were not. There were hundreds of companies of questionable repute run by "stockateers". At one point, the American Securities Exchange Commission had 256 Canadian mining companies and brokerage houses on its black list. And promotional literature from these firms mailed to the United States was returned stamped FRAUD in red ink.

In 1966, the Consumers' Association of Canada went shopping for a week's groceries for a family of five, buying such things as potatoes that needed washing and peeling, beans that needed trimming and slicing and tomatoes that weren't perfectly round. The Association's shopper spent $18.62. Then the Association bought a week's supply of packaged "convenience" foods and spent $34.87. Both shopping baskets had precisely the same nutritional value. The extra $16 bought pre-washed, instant potatoes, frozen ready-cut beans and plastic-wrapped tomatoes.

Money madness also infected the Prairies. Though Canada's share of the world wheat market was declining, harvests were still so good that a farmer who had started the 1950s almost broke was, in 1962, able to announce the arrival of his seventeenth child this way:

Mr. and Mrs. Lawrence Warken of Coronach, Saskatchewan, wish to announce the arrival at the Coronach Union Hospital of their daughter Michelle. Coming to a family blessed with a record 1962 harvest of 65,000 bushels of crop, 200 calves and 30,000 bales of feed, Michelle brings the year to a very happy conclusion.

That same year the Scandinavian Airlines System reported that trans-Atlantic bookings from rural Saskatchewan were up forty per cent—significant because a large slice of Prairie farmers are of Scandinavian origin. Prairie farmers, who knew hard times better than most, weren't saving for a rainy day, and the travel boom was happening everywhere. By 1965, we spent more on travel in the United States and abroad than we did on auto parts or food. We did much of it on credit. One bank even started a nation-wide Travelplan loan campaign.

infectious optimism

The enormous optimism that produced such spending infected even those with the least reason to be optimistic—Maritimers. In 1965, the National Employment Service announced that any area experiencing poor economic conditions would be eligible for government grants to industry and monetary aid to relocate workers where they could find jobs. Among the conditions was an average annual family income less than the national average of $5,449 and an unemployment rate twice as high as the national average. All of the Atlantic provinces qualified

While Canada from Montreal westward boomed, the Atlantic provinces still languished in the economic doldrums, and however hard provincial governments tried to attract industry, the growth rate in New Brunswick, Nova Scotia, Prince Edward Island and Newfoundland lagged behind that of the rest of the country. The search for new industries was at times desperate. In 1964, the Newfoundland government helped finance a consortium of two Newfoundlanders and fourteen Prairie ranchers, who shipped almost a thousand Herefords and Aberdeen Angus cattle east to start the Flying L Ranch on Newfoundland's Burin Peninsula boglands. Premier Joey Smallwood said the Flying L would soon have a herd of five thousand and would be competing with European producers for the Sunday roast market in Britain. Like other attempts to create new industry in Newfoundland during the decade, the Flying L was doomed to failure.

While new industries seemed incapable of taking root, old reliables were threatened. As coal gave way to oil as an energy source, Nova Scotia's centuries-old coal mines needed massive federal subsidies to stay open. By 1967, the annual subsidy amounted to $4,000 per head for every one of the 6,500 mine workers, and closure seemed likely.

heavy water

Appropriately, it was another energy industry that somehow typified the Maritime Provinces' desperate search for an economic miracle during the 1960s. In 1967, the Nova Scotia government chose the Canadian subsidiary of an American company – Deuterium – as its partner in a $120 million plant designed to supply heavy water to the increasing number of nuclear power reactors in North America. By 1969, the money was spent, and still the Glace Bay plant didn't work.

The company and the provincial and federal

Sid Barron's Nelson Canuck (. . . Nelson? What happened to Johnny and Jack, Sid? . . .) has a problem. Even his wife thinks he's getting too hot under the collar over this "independent Canada" thing. Get off your bilingual soap-box, Nelson. (Sigh!) What will the neighbors say?

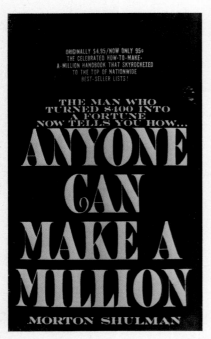

Morton Shulman, the Toronto doctor "who parlayed $400 into a fortune" by playing the stock market, made another bundle in royalties from his 1967 bestseller, Anyone Can Make A Million — *the get-rich-quick book of the decade. Based on the "surprising techniques and closely-guarded secrets of the pros" that no stockbroker would disclose, the book lured thousands of novices into the stock, bond and gold market. Appointed chief coroner of Toronto in '66, Shulman's crusading style and his almost-daily exposés of fraud, corruption and wrong-doing in high places inspired the popular weekly television series,* Wojeck.

governments were all understandably reluctant to talk about it. But the fact remained that the fantastic array of pipes and towers and retorts refused to produce one drop of heavy water, and it was costing the taxpayers of Nova Scotia – who had expected a big bonus in terms of jobs and profit – a total of $27,500 a day in maintenance and interest charges. A proposal to scrap the plant was greeted with dismay: that would mean Nova Scotia would be stuck with an annual loss of $10 million a year in paying off investors and interest until 1990. The best that experts could offer was the prediction that if governments spent another $40 million on the plant and made it work, the loss would only amount to $6 million a year. It would provide jobs, however, and so it was decided to throw in the additional $40 million.

future prospects

In 1965, in a book entitled *The Prospect of Change: Proposals for Canada's Future,* a group of University of Toronto professors wrote:

The existence of a chronically under-employed and rapidly growing population of 500,000 living permanently at subsistence levels in the rural slums of the Atlantic region can no longer be justified in the context of Canada's post-war economic growth.

They suggested that the government should launch a massive long-term programme to improve life and work prospects in the Atlantic region.

A half-million Maritimers didn't wait for government action, however; they moved out looking for their fair share of the good life other Canadians were by now taking for granted. Even so, most of them preferred to stay in Canada rather than move south to the United States, and that was a switch. For all the problems that beset the region, the decade ended with the Maritimes as optimistic about the future as the rest of the nation.

money madness

It fell to the Swedish economist Staffan B. Linder to sound a first note of warning. Linder had travelled through much of the country and, in a book entitled *The Harried Leisure Class,* concluded that the affluence – the money madness – of the 1960s had not bought happiness so much as something he called "pleasure blindness." We were, he said, either using our extra leisure to take second jobs so we could buy even more consumer goodies, or we couldn't enjoy ourselves because we felt "under some enormous pressure to do more and more exciting things with the newly-available time and money."

Money, he seemed to think, was the root of this evil. In which case, credit must certainly have been the fertilizer.

Sign Language

It seemed the whole world had been bitten by the "corporate identity" bug and was breaking out in neat, new trade marks and symbols – on products, packaging, office-fronts, letterheads and billboards. *Image* was the whole point: instant recognition in a marketplace visually cluttered with old competitors' and imitators' names and logos. The phenomenon originated in Europe, where graphic design had been regarded as a fine art since the days of Guttenberg, and arrived in Canada via multi-national corporations and foreign-born designers. And by 1967 (Expo did it), many a dowdy institution had its image scrubbed up.

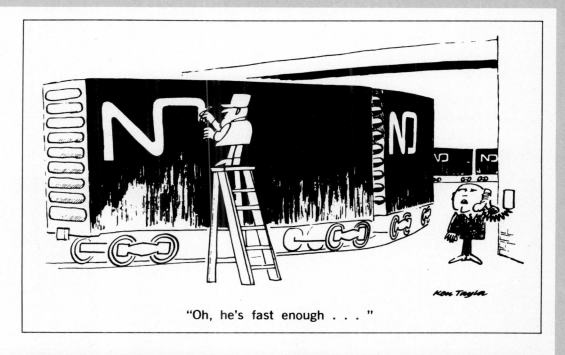

"Oh, he's fast enough . . . "

1) *Confederation Centre, Charlottetown, P.E.I.* 2) *National Arts Centre Ottawa* 3) *Ontario Pavilion, Expo 67* 4) *Bank of Montreal* 5) *Cooper & Beatty* 6) *Hydro-Québec* 7) *New Brunswick Telephone Company* 8) *Canadian National Railways* 9) *Laplante & Langevin* 10) *Canadian Pacific* 11) *Air Canada.*

For most of the fifty million people who flocked to Expo, it was the grandest exposition they were ever likely to see, and two-hour-long queues, cold foot-long hot dogs, sore feet and sky-high hotel prices did little to dampen their enthusiasm. Even the press unanimously echoed *Time* magazine's praise: "the most successful fair in history." As the host for six months of sixty-two exhibiting nations, Canada and Canadians were themselves on exhibition, and we knew we looked great.

The U.S.S.R.'s awesome display of "hardware" boasted of industrial and technical know-how. Canal-side gourmands sampled borscht and blinis.

A magnificent web of wires and lights tied together visually the various themes and levels (science, art, literature, etc.) in France's pavilion.

Buckminster Fuller's geodesic dome ("the world's biggest bubble") featured a melange of Americana some stuffy U.S. visitors thought silly and trivial:
Elvis Presley's guitar, giant blow-ups of Hollywood idols, Pop and Op Art, a replica of cowboy Tom Mix's horse, an IBM computer, a lunar-landing module . . .

Lester Pearson's last hurrah was at the Liberal convention on April 6, 1968. Backgrounded by Liberal banners and still sporting the famous bow tie his media advisors thought too folksy, in his parting remarks he quipped that Canada would expect its next PM to be "a combination of Abraham Lincoln and Batman."

CHAPTER SIX

Centennial

*Since 1967, no one has asked what it is to
be a Canadian . . . the year 1967 changed us
all profoundly, and we will never look back.*

Judy LaMarsh, *Memoirs of a Bird in a Gilded Cage,* 1968

English Canada first noticed Pierre Elliott Trudeau in November 1965, when, having just been
elected a Liberal MP from Montreal, he turned up
in the grim, grey House of Commons wearing a ca-
nary-yellow ascot and sandals. John Diefenbaker,
former Conservative prime minister and a traditional parliamentarian, all but threw a fit. He denounced Trudeau's outfit as "disrespectful" to the
House. Next day, Trudeau wore a more subdued
blue ascot.

After Pierre Trudeau became prime minister in
1968, he was inevitably compared with John F.
Kennedy, the American president who had
seemed to embody the spirit of youth and change,
and who had been assassinated in Texas on November 22, 1963. Like Kennedy, Trudeau was a
millionaire and apparently above criticism. He
was certainly not a party hack burdened with political debts. Like Kennedy, Trudeau was relatively young to be a national leader. He gave his
age as forty-six, although his sister claimed he was
forty-eight. And, again like Kennedy, he *seemed*
even younger than he was. So the new prime minister was often referred to as "Canada's Kennedy."

But the label didn't stick. It soon became clear
that Pierre Elliott Trudeau, international *bon
vivant* and jet-set ladies' man, was uniquely Canadian. And *that* brought the nation up with a start.
For so long we had measured ourselves, our institutions and our achievements against those of Britain and the United States that it was a shock – a
wonderful, slowly acknowledged shock – to realize
that at last our leaders and increasingly, our arts
and architecture and industry could be measured
against our own Canadian definitions.

For all that – Canada would be a hundred
years old in 1967 – the nation entered the decade
still tied to Britain's apron strings, with one hand
clutching at Uncle Sam's pant leg. One of our
most distinguished historians, Arthur Lower, announced with disgust that Canada was "a mere
satellite of the United States." But qualification for
admission to the financial Establishment, something of a parallel government in Canada, was, in
the words of Ottawa sociologist John Porter:
"classically Anglo-Scots ancestry, the Anglican
Church and attendance at either Upper Canada
College or Trinity College School," both institutions run along the best British boarding school
lines.

Immigration from non-Commonwealth countries at first had little impact on Canadians because non-English-speaking newcomers tended to
cluster in ethnic ghettos. It was, therefore, refresh-

*"This campaign has been the most
degrading experience of my life,"
Mike Pearson is reported to have
said at the end of the razzmatazz
campaign of '63. As if buttons and
posters and colouring books weren't
enough, wide-eyed young organizers
(aping tactics of the 1960 Kennedy
campaign in the U.S.) set up "truth
squads" to put down pro-Diefenbaker
propaganda, and on one occasion let
loose a flock of homing pigeons that
was to fly into a London, Ontario,
Liberal rally. The birds never got
there, but the Liberals did manage
to squeak out a minority victory.*

THE END OF AN ERA

When the Progressive Conservatives' "Dump Dief" cabal succeeded in unseating "the Chief" in September 1967, cartoonists like Blaine MacDonald of the Hamilton Spectator *lamented the end of an era. Who expected that jowlly face to appear in caricatures for another decade?*

ing that an inspired government publicity man, delegated in December 1960 to find Canada's two-millionth post-war immigrant, chose seventeen-year-old Annette Toft, who came from Denmark with her family to settle in Calgary. She symbolized youth and beauty and a fresh start – but she left Calgary when her parents moved on to California a year later.

It happened that way often. For many Europeans, Canada was a stop-over on the way to the United States. In the first five months of 1961, so many people moved on to the United States or returned to Europe that, on the balance sheet, Canada actually lost 14,000 people. A Toronto *Star* reporter travelled the United States, interviewing former Canadian immigrants who had moved south, and concluded: "Canada gave them no sense of belonging, of identity, so they don't feel they're losing anything by moving to greener pastures."

a new national anthem

By the time the Liberals, led by former diplomat Lester Bowles Pearson, defeated the Conservatives in the 1963 general election, however, the nation was finding itself. One reason was Pearson himself, who vowed to give us a flag of our own to replace the Union Jack, and a national anthem to supplant "God Save The Queen." Another was that pro-Commonwealth sentiment in Canada, which peaked during Britain's post-World War II woes, began to cool. However, while we didn't know what we were, we knew what we didn't want to become. And that was American.

In the 1960s, the United States appeared to be a violent and self-destructive society. Confrontations between blacks and whites in the south grew more violent and spread northward. The U.S. president was assassinated and the suspected assassin was murdered shortly thereafter in the basement of a Dallas, Texas, police station. The Americans intensified – "escalated" was the polite word – the war between North and South Vietnam, sending arms and men to the aid of successive South Vietnamese puppet regimes, each seemingly more corrupt and inept than the last. Martin Luther King, the civil rights leader who preached non-violence, was gunned down by an assassin in 1968; so was the late John Kennedy's younger brother Bobby, as he celebrated victory in a presidential primary election in California. The decade ended with urban guerilla warfare in American cities on Canada's doorstep, most notably in Detroit, Michigan, and Rochester, New York.

If we couldn't be British any more, and didn't want to be American, there was nothing left but to be Canadian. The awareness came slowly. Perhaps, as someone said afterwards, the bearskin hats worn by the honour guard on Parliament Hill were symbolic. In 1962, for the first time, the hats were made in Canada from the skins of Canadian bears; previously, they had been made in England from the skins of Russian bears.

wing-ding in Charlottetown

A more obvious harbinger of our awakening, however, was seen on Prince Edward Island. The littlest province stole a march on the rest of Canada by celebrating the Centennial three years ahead of the rest of the nation. What in fact the island commemorated in 1964, with a summer-long wing-ding of dances and picnics and horseraces, was the fact that the Fathers of Confederation first met in Charlottetown. The celebrations drew a visit from Queen Elizabeth, and alerted the rest of Canada to the fact that our one hundredth birthday was only three years away.

After decades of debate, Canada got its own maple leaf flag in time for the party. Choosing it wasn't easy, however. Politicians had been talking

"He doesn't look like a killer."

"WATCH OUT, MIKE- HE'S GOING FOR HIS GUN!"

"Unshrinkable Bob" Stanfield munching a banana in the midst of the mayhem was perhaps the most unforgetable TV image of the knock-down, drag-out PC leadership fight of '67. His duels with "Quick-Draw" Trudeau a year later earned him the barb, "Not the fastest gun in the East."

Angry letters, wild demonstrations at legion halls, a march on Ottawa (above) and six months of tedious, often asinine, debate that paralyzed Parliament were the hysterical prelude to the adoption of the Red Maple Leaf as Canada's flag. Weeks later few remembered why the fuss.

about a Canadian flag since Mackenzie King, but those who wanted one could never agree on what it should be. This time, more than two thousand organizations and individuals submitted designs for the new flag, and the controversy, first over whether we should discard the Red Ensign and, second, whether the new flag should have one maple leaf or three, was among the longest in parliamentary history. The outcome was that on February 15, 1965, at noon, the maple leaf design officially became Canada's national flag.

"The Mudslinger Affair"

In 1966, an incident of an entirely different kind helped fertilize our sense of nationhood. For decades, we had vicariously enjoyed reports of other nations' political panjandrums being caught in scandalous and sexually compromising circumstances. It was not uncommon in the United States, and British politicians seemed to make a habit of it. But it was the sort of thing that always happened somewhere else. In 1966, however, the country learned that Pierre Sévigny, who had been deputy minister of defense in the Diefenbaker government, had had an affair with Gerda Munsinger, an immigrant from Germany allegedly known to German police as a prostitute and a contact with Communist intelligence services.

During the bitter parliamentary debate someone announced that Gerda was now dead. Before the row could die down, however, Toronto *Star* reporter Robert Reguly traced Mrs. Munsinger to Munich, and she was paid thousands of dollars for her account of the relationship with Sévigny and her acquaintance with other Canadian politicians.

The debate over what came to be called "The Mudslinger Affair" went on for a year and inspired the New York *Daily News* to say that it was "pleasant to see that supposedly staid and reserved Canadians can get as excited as anyone else."

It also inspired Paul Joseph Chartier to try to blow up the House of Commons. In May 1966, he took a bomb made of two sticks of dynamite to the House, sat listening to the debate for ten minutes, then left the visitors' gallery. A few minutes later, as Hansard put it: "A loud explosion was heard in the chamber." Chartier had blown himself up with his bomb in the third floor men's room.

"a blast to wake you up"

On his body, police found a handwritten speech he had apparently hoped to make to the Commons. It read: "Mr. Speaker, Gentlemen—I might as well give you a blast to wake you up. Pearson and Diefenbaker are fighting to see who can get the most scandal on the other's party (and) for one whole year I have thought of nothing but how to eliminate as many of you as possible."

Sex and politics aside, however, what made us really proud to be Canadians was the Centennial celebration in 1967. And the star of that show was Expo '67, Montreal's world's fair, staged on a series of man-made islands in the St. Lawrence River. By virtually every definition, it was the most successful world's fair in the history of such events. A co-production of French and English Canada, with the theme "Man and His World," it drew rave reviews and fifty million visitors—twenty million more than expected. Canadians, notorious as globe-trotters who rarely visit around their own country, flocked to Montreal. The common pride that English and French Canadians found in Expo did more to unite the *deux nations* than any politician's rhetoric.

From the start, Expo was adopted by the young, who in 1967 were more exuberant than rebellious, hitch-hiking from Vancouver and Halifax to Montreal. There was a much-promoted official opening by Governor General Roland Michener on May 1, but it was what happened the next day

Even the Mounties thought she was dead. Yet The Star tracked Gerda to a chintzy Munich walk-up, opened the door and let out a story that hung on every other paper's front page for weeks. We were the first one there. The first. That's what we like to be. Especially now, for our 75th birthday. ▷ Toronto Daily Star ◁

It was the first sex scandal since the "Haggart's Whore Affair" (RAILWAYS MINISTER FOUND LIVING IN SIN WITH TYPIST) of the 1890s, and it dominated headlines throughout 1966: Gerda Munsinger, "the beautiful spy," and her affair years before with Tory deputy defence minister Pierre Sévigny.

Expo – "the jewel in Canada's Centennial crown" – not only brought the best from the world's nations together, but distracted us enough
problems and differences to show how we compared internationally. If this multi-screen, jig-saw-puzzle slide show at the Czech pavilion
queues were just as long for the NFB's Labyrinth film show on one flat/one upright screen, Ontario's circle-vision film, A Place To Stand,

when the fair opened to the public that caught the popular mood and was most widely reported: at 10:30 P.M. that chilly evening, at the Ile Ste-Hélène Expo Express subway station, a throng of teenagers, English and French and Ukrainian and Italian and whatever other kind of hyphenated Canadian was handy – all strangers to one another – spontaneously linked arms and sang "O Canada."

Expo was a government-funded, stage-managed affair. It's possible, therefore, that the celebrations organized and enjoyed by the people throughout the country were a better reflection of how Canadians felt about being Canadian. At least, that's how the federal government's Centennial Commission felt, and it awaited the start of Centennial Year with anxiety.

burning biffies

There were two symbolic flame-lighting ceremonies that New Year's Eve. One was by Prime Minister Pearson on Parliament Hill. The other was in Bowsman, Manitoba, where the citizens burned thirty-three outdoor privies. As their Centennial project, the citizens of Bowsman had installed a sewage system, but they didn't burn the biffies until Centennial Year actually began. With the temperature at -29 degrees (Fahrenheit), the United Church minister Jim Liles announced: "The time has come to bid farewell to old and beloved friends who have held up our ends throughout the years." Cliff Nowlan, town policeman and sewage plant operator, lit the bonfire, and two thousand people danced in Bowsman's five streets.

When the Centennial Commission heard about the Bowsman affair, chairman John Fisher – "Mr. Canada" they called him – sighed with relief and said: "That was the first extroverted, un-Canadian *fun* thing to happen. That was the first evidence it wasn't to be a polite, government-run party."

Come July 1, Dominion Day, there was hardly a city, town or village without a Centennial park, library, art gallery, concert hall, swimming pool or baseball diamond to dedicate. And there were community parties everywhere in a nation that celebrated as no country had done since the British went on a street party "bender" to mark the end of World War II. The citizens of St. Paul, Alberta, deserved the title Centennial Celebrants of the Year. The town had a hundred Centennial projects, including a $12,000 landing pad for flying saucers, to welcome visitors from outer space (it doubled as a bandstand), and a "Centennial Goat" auction, midway through a cattle sale. Buyers kept giving the two goats back for re-auction and they were sold seventeen times for a total of $200. The only complaint came from the last purchaser.

No one community was as zany as the individual celebrants. Two men walked from one coast of Canada to the other, one starting from Victoria and the other from Halifax. Others crossed the land by canoe, in hot-air balloons and on snowmobiles. They raced bathtubs powered by outboard motors thirty-two miles from Vancouver Island to the mainland, and two jet pilots travelled from Summerside, Prince Edward Island, to Expo '67 on water skis. At the year's end, John Fisher concluded: "I think Canadians suddenly realized the land they live in is something to brag about .... I even think that eternal search for the Canadian Identity is over. I don't know what it is yet, but I think we found it this year."

The following year – 1968 – we found the man to represent it: Pierre Elliott Trudeau.

Trudeau was of mixed French and English parentage. Independently rich and a lawyer who was said to run "a free [legal] clinic for anyone with an interesting case," he had helped spawn Quebec's "Quiet Revolution" in the 1950s – when it was simply an anti-authoritarian, anti-modernizing movement. He was outraged when the movement became separatist. He had a string of degrees from

There wasn't a cross-roads in the country that didn't have something planned for Centennial – the wierder and wilder the better. Sure, there were the official touring exhibits and performances: Festival Canada, Centennial Trains and Caravans, the Mounties' Musical Ride, and a 3,300-mile Voyageur Canoe Race from Rocky Mountain House, Alberta, to Montreal. But the bright-idea community events really celebrated the birthday best: a Giant Potlach in Burnaby, B.C.; the Yukon's Centennial Peak climb; a public Biffy Bonfire in Bowsman, Man.; a Gaelic Mod Festival at St. Ann's, Cape Breton; an All-You-Can-Eat Oyster Feast at Tyne Valley, P.E.I.; the Steeves Family's 200th Annual Reunion at Hillsborough, N.B. What did you say you were doing?

Who's minding their calories? Probably no one was the day the Queen sliced into the biggest birthday cake ever made in Canada for the official Centennial ceremonies on Parliament Hill.

the University of Montreal, Harvard, the Sorbonne and the London School of Economics. He was a skin-diver, a skier, and an absolutely appalling pianist. He had toured the world, both as a footloose student and as an official visitor from Canada; in the latter role he once startled Chinese tour guides by turning a somersault during a particularly boring official tour. He was once caught throwing snowballs at a statue of Stalin in Moscow while attending an economists' conference.

When Lester Pearson resigned in 1968, the Liberals chose Trudeau to replace him. At the leadership convention, he defeated half a dozen party strongmen, among them Paul Martin who had been in politics for thirty-two years. Withdrawing from the leadership race, Martin wrote: "I have been caught in the generation gap." He didn't make that statement public, but he should have, because that's precisely what had happened. The party was as infected by youth fever as the rest of the country proved to be when Trudeau called his first election in June 1968.

"It's Spring"

Wherever he went he drew crowds undreamed of by other politicians. Kissing Trudeau became a national female ambition. Women – not just teenagers, but mature women as well – broke through police cordons to touch him. They called it Trudeaumania and Trudolatry. He promised little ("I have this peculiar ability to be wrong sometimes"). Teenagers too young to vote – voting age was then twenty-one – campaigned for him, wearing buttons that simply said: "It's Spring." Pierre Elliott Trudeau was young, the product of both founding races, an untainted newcomer to politics at a time when established politicians were condemned for the problems of the world.

The winter of '67 - '68 was the "hottest" time in Pierre Trudeau's pre-election career. Two weeks before he announced his candidacy, 600 prominent French and English supporters launched a "Draft Trudeau" petition that cut across all party lines. (NDP faithful, Pierre Berton – then the better-known Pierre – was among the first to sign.) During the June election campaign, "Trudeaumania" was busting out all over. This near-riot was at a rally at Toronto's Royal York.

Trudeaumania

His every movement was a "happening"; his every word a pearl; his every prank a front-page feature; his every quip a headline. At the April leadership convention in Ottawa, crowds twice as large as the other candidates could muster trailed after him. A month later, jetting from St. John's to Victoria, otherwise sensible young women pushed and shoved to touch the hem of his garment and (Wow!) maybe even get a kiss. This was "Trudeaumania."

While other candidates moved through the convention behind paid bands and parades of chanting, sign-waving fans, Trudeau sat-out the hoopla, mobbed by the press, TV cameras and microphones. When the final ballot was announced (Trudeau 1,203; Winters 954; Turner 195), the arena erupted in pandemonium. "Like a wave-smashing storm . . . the roar of the cheering never seems to stop. Trudeau reaches the platform. A brief silence, his first words, and it starts again."

It wasn't only a "teenybopper" phenomenon. Artists Joyce Wieland and Michael Snow formed a Canadians Abroad for Trudeau Committee in New York and threw a lavish party for him during a visit. The attaché case above is Gord Rayner's Trudeau Bag – *a whimsical creation the Toronto artist put together to "bag" the elusive* PM *in '68, after he and Graham Coughtry spent days trying to track down the vacationing Trudeau on the jet-set's Spanish island of Ibiza.*

LIVING AND LEARNING

The Hall-Dennis Commitee's Living and Learning *report on Ontario's educational aims and objectives recommended over 250 changes (many of them radical) to the system. The Cameron, Chant and Parent commissions, which had tackled problems in Alberta, B.C. and Quebec, urged similar reforms.*

CHAPTER SEVEN

Living and Learning

*The constant buzz of the teacher's voice to
a tongue-tied captive audience was accepted
as desirable practice. However, in the light
of present-day experience, the lecture method,
used alone . . . is far too restricting.*

Hall-Dennis Committee, *Living and Learning,* 1968

In September 1969, Anne MacDonald of Moncton, New Brunswick, and Colleen Tambling of Campbell River, British Columbia, were both seventeen. Both wore their hair long as was the fashion. Both were about to enter grade twelve. Both thought Pierre Trudeau was "neat" and both admitted to liking the Beatles but secretly thought the Rolling Stones were . . . well, more exciting.

In Moncton, Anne MacDonald returned to school and a rigorously scheduled day in which she marched in single file and in silence from classroom to classroom. In Campbell River, Colleen Tambling went back to class, lit a cigarette and, when the first period ended, decided to skip art and go for a walk instead.

At the end of a decade in which enormous amounts of time and money and energy were spent on education, Canadian schools, colleges and universities were in hopeless disagreement about what to teach, and how to teach it. Anne MacDonald's school in Moncton and Colleen Tambling's in Campbell River represented the po-larized extremes of what we did to our children – from telling them when they could blow their noses through to letting them treat school as though it were the gang clubhouse.

It is hardly surprising that education was a public obsession during the 1960s. When the decade began there were three million kids in school; when Anne MacDonald and Colleen Tambling started their grade twelve year, there were *six* million. We spent more on education than we ever had on any single enterprise, war excepted: the 1969 education bill was more than $6 billion, or better than ten per cent of our total income. The children of the post-war baby boom were the offspring of the second richest society in human history, and we were determined to give them the best schooling money could buy. Trouble was, no one was sure what we were schooling them for. The pace of change was so fast that it left everyone floundering, parents most of all.

Technology and the knowledge explosion had caused most of the problem. By mid-decade, new scientific knowledge was becoming available so fast that college students then acquiring professional qualifications faced the prospect of going back to school for catch-up courses at least three times during their careers. At the same time, high school students were being told that automation was changing industry and commerce so fast that no matter what job they took, they'd probably be

*The educational cloud raining down
course "core textbooks" and 19th-
century English novels passed by
the end of the decade as schools
adopted "discovery, exploration and
inquiry" methods in teaching. A-V
(audio-visual) equipment became a
natural element in the learning
process. Percentage marks and grade
levels were abandoned by some boards.
And daily homework was replaced by
individual or group term projects.*

Fraternities were still "in" on campuses in the early-'60s when this blanket-toss took place at a Queen's-Varsity football game. No protests, just a little rowdyism, bonhomie and boozing.

displaced by machines and have to change occupations five times before they retired. Worse, government experts estimated that by 1969 jobs would be disappearing at the rate of two for every one potential worker leaving school or college. True, economists said this meant we'd still be rich, so no depression was expected, but it sounded as though we were headed for a world in which work wasn't vital for survival, and a labour market in which it would be better to be a Jack-of-all-trades than master of one.

In response to these changes, two warring educational philosophies long familiar in private schools spilled over into the public system. One philosophy was seen as the preserve of the young and the radical, those who protested that the old ways were bad ways. The principal of Colleen Tambling's school in Campbell River symbolized this group. His students learned more or less what they wanted, at their own pace and in their own way. Teachers were not authority figures; they were "resource persons" on hand to dispense knowledge when asked, and to guide pupils who were "discovering" knowledge.

The opposite philosophy held that you could lead students to the well of knowledge, but you couldn't make them drink, and so structure and discipline were necessary to provide the secure framework within which the young were free to learn.

The battle was for nothing less than the minds of the young, and thus the shape of the future. "Discovery" education, which gave the young freedom of choice and taught them to live rather than work, was seen as a first faltering step toward Utopia. Structured education was condemned as a tool of the capitalist Establishment, designed to raise a generation suitably respectful of authority, while producing so many neurosurgeons and so many short order cooks, depending on the needs of the economy.

At the beginning of the decade, the government's greatest concern was how poorly the young were educated. One federal government report revealed that Canada had two million "functional illiterates"; that 200,000 Canadians had never even been to school; and that seven million of the twenty million population had not completed high school. And this was in a work marketplace where General Motors wouldn't hire an errand boy at their Ontario or Quebec offices unless he had an Ontario grade twelve or Quebec grade eleven education.

At the height of this concern the baby boom began to overload the junior schools. "Portable" classrooms began to appear outside schools in towns and cities across Canada. There were never enough buildings for the students. In Ontario, for example, nine new universities were built during the decade, and they were woefully overcrowded by 1969. Hundreds of community colleges, a notch above high schools and one below universities, were built throughout the country, partly to meet the demand for higher education, and partly to keep the young out of a labour market that couldn't absorb them.

Battles about what the young should be taught persisted throughout the decade. It wasn't until 1965 that teachers in Alberta were permitted to mention Darwin's theories of evolution in their high school biology courses. And even though the taboo was lifted that year, the provincial department of education still insisted students be told: "To most people the formation of the world was an act of special creation controlled by God. There is no evidence this was not so." In 1960, also in Edmonton, school trustee Mrs. Edith Rogers opposed a course on sex and family life, calling it a "communist inspired attack on moral standards."

But the real excitement was in the philosophy of education, and it emerged quietly in Saskatchewan in 1964, where the provincial education

Student-power activist? Hardly. This theology student is practice-preaching the old gospel. Except for a few "Ban-the-Bomb pinkos," most students then fretted about exams and marks.

In September 1968, twenty Queen's undergrads pitched their tents on university principal John Deutsch's lawn to protest the student housing shortage in Kingston, Ontario. The word got around fast. A week later, the radical fringe of the U of T's Student's Administrative Council urged hard-up apartment seekers to set up housekeeping on campus lawns. The protest ended when cops moved in and sent the tent-dwellers packing.

To accommodate the massive population bulge of the post-war "baby boom," provinces pumped millions into high school construction in the fifties, and more millions into colleges with huge, 200-seat lecture halls like this in the sixties.

department said children should learn at their own pace and began eliminating grades and examinations so that students did not have to compete, did not have to measure their success or failure by the definitions of others. It was in Saskatchewan that the little red schoolhouse first began to disappear, or at least change. Traditionally, one or two teachers had coped with kids from kindergarten through to grade eight – in the same building and often in the same classroom. With astonishing unanimity educators and governments agreed this was le. than ideal and set up regional high schools fed by fleets of yellow buses that scooped up the young from miles around. Farm kids would often have to catch the bus at 7:30 A.M. to be at school by 9:00 o'clock. It was such a circumstance that led to the rebellion in Endeavour, Saskatchewan.

At the start of the 1967-68 term, the villagers of Endeavour refused to send their children to the re-

gional school twenty-five miles away, and set up their own school in the village library. More important, their school had grades and exams. Teachers, too, were often unenthusiastic. Six years after introducing the system, Saskatchewan education authorities reported: "The system is working quite well, though not all teachers are accustomed to it."

By that time, however, Saskatchewan's experiments in gradeless teaching paled when measured against what seemed, from published reports, to be a nationwide passion for the "new" education. The focus for the publicity was the 1968 report of an Ontario provincial committee on education. Called *Living and Learning*, the report soon became internationally known as the Hall-Dennis Report, named for co-chairmen Judge Emmett Hall and high school principal Lloyd Dennis. The large multi-coloured, expensive-looking report

"Doing their own thing," 350 high school pupils taught themselves and each other in a York University experiment SEED *(Summer of Experience, Exploration and Discovery). Critics called the approach "the blind leading the blind."*

"I WONDER WHAT IT WAS LIKE WHEN PEOPLE HAD TO LEARN BY HAND?"

While school boards were spending thousands of dollars on electronic language lab machines, projectors, tape recorders and instructional hardware, teachers' colleges were busy training next year's graduates to use the new-fangled devices. In one school, an unsuspecting snoop opened a cupboard door, only to find the place crammed with brand-new, untouched equipment. When he asked the principal why the stuff was just sitting there, the reply was, "Well, nobody seems to want to use it."

sold for $4, advocated the abolition of all grades, exams and structured curricula, and proposed that they be replaced with a twelve-year "learning experience" in which students proceeded at their own pace to "discover" knowledge.

The report was important because it dissected, accepted or rejected most of the educational theories propounded during the previous half century. The committee heard briefs from more than a hundred interested groups including a class of grade eight students who told them: "We think we learn best when we study what we want to study."

Ontario's educational structure was seen as fairly typical of those in all western democracies. The Hall-Dennis Report, therefore, had a massive impact when it concluded that the student "is expected to be stuffed and programmed like a computer at any hour of the school day and to be filled with enthusiasm for every golden nugget cast in

his direction." It added: "If the child fails to benefit from the curriculum provided, the assumption often made is that the fault lies with him and he is a misfit."

The sort of education advocated by Hall-Dennis was first available in so-called open-plan junior schools. Allendale Heights Public School in Barrie, Ontario, was among the first of these to be built. There were no classrooms as such, just broadloomed "learning areas," each of which accommodated three grades. There were no desks, just a litter of occasional tables for kids who needed them. There were no school periods, no formal lessons and little discipline. In one area at any moment, you'd find kids simultaneously studying math, spelling, geography, history, modelling in clay, building a dolls' house with popsicle sticks, playing with tape recorders, listening to records or just curled up on the carpet under a table reading.

Such educational anarchy was hard on traditionally trained teachers. That was one reason junior high and high schools were more resistant to "democratization." And where they were too slow to change, the kids protested. The ultimate protest was a school in Vancouver called Know Place. Its name was a pun on the Greek word "Utopia," which means "no place."

Know Place

Sonia Makaroff, sixteen, daughter of a university lecturer, said Know Place was set up because the traditional high school was "so repressive that one of us was always in trouble for the way we dressed or wore our hair or for asking questions instead of just parroting back the teachers' answers." The school existed in the Fourth Avenue hippie area of Vancouver and, surprisingly, had the blessing of the provincial department of education which rented textbooks to the students. Unknowingly echoing Hall-Dennis, fifteen-year-old pupil Marion Campbell said: "We're learning to be, not just to do."

Universities were even more resistant than high schools to pressures for this new "education for living." University radicals who tried to duplicate the Know Place example ran into trouble. In mid-decade a group of young teachers and graduate students at the University of Toronto decided that traditional university structures should be abandoned in favour of "an environment where individuals and groups can create their own experience." With federal government loans, they built the eighteen-storey Rochdale College on Toronto's Bloor Street.

Rochdale opened in the summer of 1968 as part student-residence, part open-college. Fifty "learn as you please" educational courses were offered, ranging from film to oriental religion, silk screening and printing, mathematics and philosophy. Within twelve months the "college" had become a slum that consistently failed to pass city public health inspections. Rochdale was a drug centre, openly boasting its own laboratories where LSD could be tested for purity. Many residents failed to pay their rent. At first there was no board of governors, just open meetings at which consensus conclusions were to be reached. At Rochdale's peak, one such meeting lasted eight hours, the consensus decision being to defer reaching a consensus until another meeting was called by consensus.

fantasies of a liberal society

By the fall of 1969, when ex-idealist general manager Bernie Bowmers quit with an ulcer, the college actually elected a council which promptly decided the place should be sold because hardly anyone had paid rent and Rochdale was broke. Dennis Lee said he and his co-founders displayed "intense naiveté" in thinking Rochdale could run on freedom. "We failed on our own grounds, not because anybody did us in," he said. Howard Adelman, another founder, said: "Rochdale is really living out the fantasies of a liberal society."

At the start of the decade there were 114,000 students in Canadian universities. Nine years later there were twice as many universities and three times as many students. And campus protests had become almost a spectator sport.

In 1968, the radicals took control of the Canadian Union of Students, and the president, Peter Warrian, twenty-five, told members: "Everyone is saying that this is the year we really sock it to administrators, burn down their buildings if necessary." It was the start of a power battle.

That year, ten of the twenty-three newly-founded *Collèges d'enseignement général et professionnel* – Quebec's tuition-free colleges which offered pre-university courses and three-year business and technical programmes – were invaded and

Students determined to have a voice in all university-run affairs set up off-campus co-op bookstores to bite into the age-old monopolies of authorized, college-run outlets. Viewing their every action as part of a "world-wide liberation movement," they plastered the picture of Cuban revolutionary Ché Guevara on dorms, protest posters and ads.

Opposite page: *Posing in front of a sculpture titled* Unknown Student *on the sidewalk of their 18-storey concrete co-op, Rochdale College fund-raisers are about to set off on a last-ditch trip to bail out their bankrupt "free university." Completed in the fall of 1968 as an unstructured and "hassle-free" alternative to the University of Toronto around the corner, a year of drug raids, tenants' bad debts and vandalism (much of it by drop-in "drop-outs") touched off a smear campaign that condemned Rochdale as "a high-rise Sodom and Gomorrah" and "the world's biggest drugstore."*

DANIEL JOHNSON DESCENDANT DU MONT SINAÏ

Plagued for nearly a century with an absurdly complex, bureaucratic and parochial system of education, the new, centralized (since 1964) Quebec Ministry of Education faced its first test of strength in the spring of 1967, when, after a five-month teachers' strike, Premier Daniel Johnson brought down Bill 25, ordering 70,000 teachers back to work and suspending their right to strike. Teachers retaliated with rotating walk-outs for more than two years until a contract (their first) was signed in November '69.

occupied for more than a week. The student grievances included shortages of job openings, the internal administration of the CEGEPs, and the shortage of university places for CEGEP graduates. At Simon Fraser University in Burnaby, British Columbia, more than a hundred students took over the administration offices to protest too rigorous admission standards, and refused to move until carried out bodily by the RCMP.

army units on stand-by

In Montreal, McGill University students disrupted campus life with demonstrations and sit-ins that won them seats on the university senate and representation on committees that appoint professors. Still dissatisfied, in March 1969 more than five thousand Montreal students mounted a demonstration to protest authoritarian education and English domination of the economy, and worried city fathers persuaded Ottawa to put army units on stand-by, ready to restore order if needed.

At the University of British Columbia, radicals occupied the faculty club for twenty-two hours. At the University of New Brunswick, officials had to call in the police to quell one student rebellion. Fearing trouble, five smaller schools (Alberta, Manitoba, Lethbridge, Ryerson in Toronto and Carleton in Ottawa) each gave students seats on their Boards of Governors before they were asked to do so.

Only one Canadian incident, however, remotely paralleled the pitched battles at European and American colleges. And it was seen not only as another student drama, but also as a demonstration of the impotence that everyone was beginning to feel in the 1960s in the face of institutions grown too big for people, and of machines that reduced human destiny to a punch-card programmed predictability.

In 1969, at Montreal's Sir George Williams

University, six black students from the West Indies made an allegation that an assistant professor of biology was a racist. When students failed to convince administrators that their charges were justified, they led a hundred or more radicals to the university computer centre where they stayed behind barricades for fourteen days demanding a new hearing of their allegations. When it was finally refused, they systematically gutted the building, burning and destroying the $2 million computer centre.

"Go, cops, go"

When police led the vandals to paddy wagons, a thousand or more students watched, chanting: "Go, cops, go." A year earlier they would have called the cops "pigs." But it was now 1969, and moderate students were beginning to clip the wings of the radicals who had just months earlier been student movement leaders. At the University of Toronto, radicals denounced president Claude Bissell's administration for "duplicity, dishonesty and a general disregard for students and their interests." Shocked, the great mass of students—until now largely apathetic—circulated a petition supporting Bissell.

That same year, world-renowned anthropologist and behaviourist Margaret Mead pointed out that only in primitive societies did the children grow up so obsessed with the struggle for sheer survival that they lived like their parents. In advanced societies, she said, children readily abandon their parents' ways. Of the protesting youth of the 1960s, Mead said:

Like children of wilderness pioneers, they're the first natives in the New World. For the first time in human history there are no elders anywhere who know what the young people know. The generation gap will only be closed when parents let their children teach them what the real issues and questions are.

Montreal police lean into a mob of students and outside agitators during the February 1969 Sir George Williams University riot. Whipped up by a handful of black West Indian students over the alleged racism of a biology professor (later cleared by an impartial committee), a group of self-styled "guerillas" (both Whites and Blacks) mindlessly set fire to the 16-storey Hall Building and destroyed the $2.5 million Computer Centre. Eight were tried and deported.

Fashion Revolution

No fashion theory explains the seemingly arbitrary changes in clothing design as convincingly as the "Erotic Principle."
And in no previous period did style conspire to seduce as it did in the sixties. The couturiers' inventory itself
makes the point: mini-skirts, bodystockings, "no-bra" brassieres, see-through blouses, topless swimsuits, "nude" lipstick.
But there was a broader significance to the fashion revolution, as well. By 1969, the hemline had plunged from micro to maxi,
the unisex look was in, and pants suits had arrived. The sex fling was over, and women began dressing for the man's world.

Demure young women opted for versions of this crocheted mini-dress with a flesh-tone lining.

The bikini, first seen in the late-fifties, dominated beaches in ever-skimpier styles.

The maxi-coat and the maxi-skirt signalled the hemline's drop in '68 but had fleeting appeal.

In ten short years, the hemline made its daring ascent, from the early-'60s A-line dress to the micro. By necessity designers invented pantyhose.

The free-and-easy, anything-goes Mod Look of the late-'60s made anything unexpected fashionable — pants, vests, shirts, ties . . . women's liberation?

Place Ville-Marie (the 42-storey white marble building at left) towers against a skyline of skyscrapers that rose after its completion in 1962, some of them linked by underground shopping promenades. Before work began, the pit-yards of the Canadian National Railways (known as "The Hole") occupied the site.

CHAPTER EIGHT

Downtown

*I have not yet relearned what every city
dweller has to do in self-protection – that is,
to block out of sight and hearing some of the
zoom and flash and screech and rush and buzz
and boing and shove and clatter.*

Margaret Laurence, "Love and Madness in the City,"
Vancouver Sun, November 15, 1969

William Zeckendorf and Eric McLean. Two men
more different in occupation and lifestyle would
have been hard to find in Canada in 1960. Zeckendorf, millionaire tycoon, was a living symbol of the
"big and new and therefore better" school of
thought that dominated life in the first half of the
decade. McLean, a music critic, represented the
opposing but less popular "it's old so it must be
good" camp. Yet these two men, and the passions
that propelled them to accomplish what many
considered impossible, help explain how the face
of Canada came to be changed

When the 1960s began, Canada lagged behind
the rest of North America and much of Europe in
post-war city planning and development. True,
our suburbs were wondrous places. Built through
the 1950s, they offered the split-level ranch-type
life that, for a while at least, fulfilled most
Canadians' dreams of property and possessions.
They represented a sort of paradise, and none so
much as Etobicoke, an upper-middle-class suburb
of Toronto, where local aldermen actually set
about legislating the lifestyle of this Valhalla.

By mid-decade, Etobicoke bylaws required
loyal Etobicoke homeowners to cut the grass at
least once a week; to keep front hedges and fences
under two-and-a-half feet high; to use air conditioners that made no more than sixty decibels of
measurable noise; to refrain from building backyard bird houses. It was the first community in
Canada to demand that garbage be placed in plastic bags for collection – "gift-wrapped garbage," it
was called. For a while the council even debated
the wisdom of setting a maximum temperature for
household bath water, and ordering that there be a
wastebasket in every room. As Reeve John MacBeth said: "If people don't like the restrictions
they can move to the country."

Trouble was, the reverse was happening. People were flooding to the cities from the country so
fast that by 1966, 73.6 per cent of the nation's population lived in towns or cities. The attraction was
money. There was more of it in cities and towns.
There was, however, precious little else in the city
centres. Even the boosterish Vancouver *Sun* said
of its own downtown:

*It's no fun to walk around in, and it's becoming intolerable to drive around in. It is, in short, an area designed for work, not pleasure. It is an area people'd
by citizens who wish they were somewhere else.*

**Relative population sizes of Canada's
Metropolitan areas 1967**

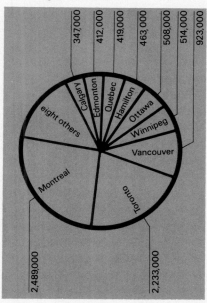

*The population shift from rural to
urban areas that began at the time
of Confederation continued unabated.
In 1867, less than 20% of the total
population of 3.5 million lived in
cities. A century later over 75%
was crammed into metropolitan areas.*

Block by block, old houses and office buildings crumbled to dust at the wrecker's ball, replaced by non-descript apartments. For rent: a room with a view ... of other rooms with views ...

When that was written – April 1963 – you could have said much the same of almost every city centre in Canada. Indeed, Toronto so lacked character and individuality, was so typically a North American mid-western city, that American town planner Vincent dePonte said that going to Toronto from Cleveland or Cincinnati was like "arriving at the place you just left."

Cities south of the border had seen a flurry of redevelopment during the 1950s. Whole city cores had been ripped out, and old buildings replaced with glittering new highrises. By contrast, in 1960 downtown Canada was by and large grey, grubby and rundown. The exception, of course, was Montreal. Montreal had William Zeckendorf.

Zeckendorf was an American developer responsible for major projects from Washington, D.C. to Denver, Colorado. His credo was: "It is not only socially desirable *but also economically sound* to aim for the highest possible standards in planning, architecture and construction." More bluntly, the better the architecture and construction, the more rent you can charge and the bigger the ultimate profits.

The seven-acre, three-block wasteland that fronted on Dorchester Street was owned by Canadian National Railways. By the time Zeckendorf found it, CN president Donald Gordon had already decided the land should start making money. CN leased the land to Zeckendorf's company, which first set about building a new railway station and a hotel – to be called the Queen Elizabeth – and then developed the site in the most spectacular manner he could. The result was the forty-two-storey $86 million cruciform-shaped Place Ville-Marie.

After five years of building, it was formally opened in September 1962, but its effect was noticeable elsewhere far earlier. By 1961, another massive Montreal development, Place Victoria, was in the planning stage, and the status game demanded that it be higher than Place Ville-Marie –

forty-five storeys. Soon the traditional rivalry between Montreal and Toronto reared its head and the Toronto-Dominion Bank announced that it, too, would build a massive complex consisting of three buildings which would occupy at least one city block, so that "a downgrade area of downtown Toronto will be turned into a thing of beauty." What's more, said Toronto-Dominion, the TD Centre would have one building that was fifty-four storeys high.

skyscrapers on the prairies

And so it went across the country. By 1965, we were launched on an orgy of demolishing the old and constructing the towering new. The first "skyscraper" on the prairies – the twenty-storey Elvedon House in Calgary – wasn't opened until 1961; but five years later even Regina, surrounded by nothing but land, boasted highrise apartment towers on the edge of wheatfields. In Ottawa, twenty-two acres of blighted downtown around the Parliament buildings were designated for redevelopment. In Saskatoon, the railway moved out of the city centre and work began on redeveloping the twenty-four vacated, acres. The railway also moved in Moncton, and a thirty-store shopping centre went up in its place.

Sometimes this urban renewal was unquestionably desirable. Halifax razed the north-end shantytown called Africville and relocated its residents – all of them Blacks – in public housing as well designed as anything of its kind in the country. But even in that there was evidence of the gulf between planners' dreams and people's needs. The housing project was well-maintained, the lawns were neatly curried and everything was painted a blinding white – and the former shanty dwellers hated it. "I really miss the closeness we Africville people had," said Mrs. Althea Mantley after three years in what, after Africville, should have seemed a four-bedroom palace.

This redevelopment of Canadian cities, more obvious at first in the east than the west, was orchestrated almost totally by non-Canadians. Zeckendorf was American and his architects were I.M. Pei Associates of New York, who were later to mastermind a dozen or so other Zeckendorf projects in Canada, including the redevelopment of downtown Edmonton. Place Victoria, of Italian design and built down the street from Place Ville-Marie, was backed by the Dutch-owned Mercantile Bank of Canada and Italy's *Societa Generale Immobilaire*. American architect Mies van der Rohe designed the massive Toronto-Dominion Centre. Toronto's oyster-shaped City Hall, which got rave notices in the world's press when it opened in 1965, was designed by a Finn Viljo Revell. And the project that could ultimately prove to be the most exciting of all – the Wascana downtown development in Regina – was conceived by a Japanese-American architect, Minoru Yamasaki.

a hundred-year plan

In 1962, the Saskatchewan government and the Regina city council, conscious of the fact that, with government control, city design could be used to enrich the human spirit, set up an autonomous Wascana Centre Authority with complete control over one-and-a-half square miles of lakeshore land in which Regina's downtown would slowly be built. It was a hundred-year plan for a city that architect Yamasaki decided would ultimately have a population of around 500,000.

Outsiders not only planned most of the cityscape for Canada's second century, they also financed it. Local developer Charles McCulloch was unable to raise a $16 million mortgage for a major highrise development in Halifax. "Upper Canada, where the money is, had no faith in Halifax." McCulloch said in 1969 at the opening

With a few insignificant changes, this ad could have run in any city newspaper across the country, and the rental office phones would have started ringing. The scarcity of other accommodation, and the thrill for young singles of being in the "swinging city," were reason enough to sign now and fret over rent later.

of the Scotia Square. The complex was built with the aid of a mortgage readily raised in New York.

vanishing landmarks

City skylines changed with disconcerting speed; old familiar landmarks vanished, often before anyone could mount a campaign to save them, and were replaced by shining shafts of glass or pre-stressed concrete. With few exceptions, the new buildings were cold, uncomfortable monuments either to an architect's ego or the corporate pride of a bank or business. In this, they were similar to Zeckendorf's Place Ville-Marie. There, in the main lobby, there were no seats, no paintings, no sculptures, in fact, no signs that human beings were even welcome. The Royal Bank of Canada had its headquarters in one wing of the cruciform shape and its main floor area, where people spend little time, was the most impressive public space of all, while the main "people place" – the basement level that contained more than fifty stores, several restaurants and two movie theatres – seemed claustrophobic.

This kind of commercial development had an immediate impact on housing. The newly urban, mobile society contained a high proportion of young people who worked in the new city centres and demanded rental accommodation near their jobs. Whole neighbourhoods were demolished to make way for highrise apartment buildings. This was most apparent in the English Bay area of Vancouver. There a forest of highrise apartment blocks shot up, so similar in design and surroundings that they might have sprung whole from the same architect's plans. In Toronto, where the housing towers were more numerous but more widely distributed, one construction boss said that by 1966 he didn't need architects because he could build a forty-storey apartment building from memory.

The peril, then, was that cities that were be-coming intimidating, arid downtown commercial areas ringed by highrise apartments, vertical villages where tenants were transient, lonely and lacking in any sense of belonging to a community.

This is where Eric McLean, musician and music critic for the Montreal *Star* came in. He led what was at first one of the most unco-ordinated but effective people's protests in Canadian history. In 1961, when Place Ville-Marie was half-built, McLean leased a four-storey flophouse on Bonsecours Street in the historic but rundown Old Town. This particular building was, in fact, the former townhouse of the nineteenth century leader Louis-Joseph Papineau. Within eighteen months, McLean had painstakingly restored one floor of the house and taken up his option to buy the building for $25,000.

make way for parking lots

"I'm not an eccentric," he said. "The city is in danger of reaching inhuman proportions. The new buildings are all monstrous, and all around the Old Quarter I can see buildings that are basically beautiful being torn down to make way for parking lots and commercial development. Yet it is one of the few places where you have an harmonious style of architecture that is human in scale. That's why I moved in to a place as important as the Papineau house and started renovating. I hope other people will follow suit."

They did. By 1963, Montreal's city council had designated the Old Town an historic area, put in streetlights based on century-old designs and even restored the sidewalks and cobbled streets. And at about the same time people across Canada took up McLean's lead. In Vancouver, a city where redevelopment came late in the decade, young entrepreneurs invaded the slum area known as Gastown and turned several streets of decrepit warehouses, hotels and junk stores into the smart-

The rapid increase in jet use for travel and transport between cities brought into question the viability of Canada's railroads. As service on small-town spur-lines was cut, and government support shifted to long-haul trucking, three railway workers' unions banded together in '69 to lobby for a government STOP.

Opposite page: *Vancouver's building "boom" of the fifties saw dozens of apartment high-rises crop up along the beaches of English Bay (left), and in the sixties, acres of downtown property were razed for office and residential towers. Vancouver architect Arthur Erickson, the man behind many of the magnificent public buildings, refuted much of the skepticism about cities when he said: "Everything we've enjoyed in western civilization, we owe to cities."*

"We're lucky here, you know," said American urbanologist Jane Jacobs, after she moved to Canada in the summer of '68 to take up a teaching post at Toronto's York University. "We can look down and see what's going wrong in New York and Cleveland and then try to avoid the same thing happening here. But it's not easy, because the same destructive forces are at work in Canada." The author of two controversial books on urban problems (The Death and Life of Great American Cities *and* The Economy of Cities)*, she was one of the fiercest opponents of the* Spadina Expressway *(see page 100).*

est boutique and restaurant area north of San Francisco.

The market for old houses in or near the city centre began to boom. The most frequently cited example of so-called middle-class "white painters" taking over and renovating working-class inner-city neighbourhoods was Macpherson Avenue in Toronto, a street of modest Victorian brick homes. In 1960, one such terrace house might have cost $12,000 at most. By 1967 the same house had been through the hands of the renovators and had one large living-dining room, and a labour-saving kitchen on the ground floor, new plumbing and wiring, and stripped-down varnished pine trim. The old front porch was gone; there were decorative but non-functional shutters on the windows and the brickwork had been either sandblasted or white-painted. The house, perhaps formerly owned by a retired CPR brakeman or a factory worker, was now worth $40,000 and was occupied by an upwardly mobile lawyer, ad-man, television producer or stockbroker in his thirties with two kids and a wife grown bored with the suburbs.

liveable cities

The efforts of the new inner-city people were so successful that after urban planner Jane Jacobs, author of *Death and Life of Great American Cities*, visited Toronto she wrote in the New York *Times* that as cities go "Toronto really works," and promptly moved north to live there. Americans who lived in border states became envious; the Greyhound bus company even ran bus tours from various points in the United States to see Canada's liveable cities. In October 1969, Edmonton published a promotional booklet in which it boasted of the "little freedoms" that Edmontonians still enjoyed but which "a lot of North Americans only remember with fondness." Those freedoms included being able to take a business trip or vacation without fearing that "race riot or civil disobedience will threaten your home," and of knowing that street crimes and violence "are a rarity rather than a daily occurrence."

Much of the vitality of the city cores came from the young. Those same apartment complexes spawned a new lifestyle that seemed glamorous. Newer apartment buildings boasted their own swimming pools, sauna baths, recreation rooms, laundromats and often, in the basement, the equivalent of the corner cigar store. Tennis and squash courts were not uncommon. Toronto's multi-building St. James Town development, on the edge of the city centre, actually employed a social director and games organizer,

urban alienation

Such facilities were designed to fend off loneliness, promote togetherness, and help boy meet girl and vice versa. Yet psychiatrists and social workers regarded urban alienation – the social scientists' term for loneliness – as a major social problem spawned by highrise living. People rarely knew who lived next door or across the corridor. "It takes courage to make the first gesture of friendliness for fear of being rebuffed," said the St. James Town social director. "Besides, it may turn out to be someone you can't stand and you're stuck virtually living with them."

Meanwhile, back in Montreal's Old Town, Eric McLean was having no such problems. His old flophouse was now the focal point of a showplace neighbourhood. Instead of being lonely, McLean complained that there were too many tourists come to gaze in admiration. He also found that what had been described by others as his insanity had left him, on paper at least, unexpectedly wealthy. The old Papineau house had cost him $25,000 in 1962. In 1969, it was valued at $200,000. William Zeckendorf had by then gone broke.

The last bolt—a gold-plated one—in place, high-steel workers atop the roof beams of the 56-floor Toronto Dominion Centre doff hats, celebrating completion of their work in April 1966. Among this group are several Mohawk Indians, famous for their skyscraper work since New York's Empire State Building.

Sixteen years of haggling over the effects of the Spadina Expressway came to a head in November 1969, when "people power" protesters organized to kill the on-again/off-again project for good. Critics, such as Jane Jacobs (see page 98), argued that construction would destroy mid-town neighborhoods and create slums.

CHAPTER NINE

People Power

It sometimes seems to Indians that Canada shows more interest in preserving its rare whooping cranes than its Indians. Indians hold no grudge against the big, beautiful nearly extinct birds, but we would like to know how they managed their deal.

Harold Cardinal, *The Unjust Society*, 1969

Shopping one Saturday in the spring of 1966, Mrs. June O'Reilly was asked to pay $1.20 for a solitary turnip at her local supermarket. Admittedly, turnips were out of season in Canada; this one came from Florida or California or some other kindlier clime. But $1.20 for one turnip! An outraged Mrs. O'Reilly paid for the vegetable, gift-wrapped it and mailed it to Prime Minister Lester Pearson with a demand that he do something about the outrageous cost of food. When that fact became public – Mrs. O'Reilly not being one to avoid publicity – it provided a focus for a nationwide consumers' revolt that had already begun in Newfoundland.

A few months earlier, Mrs. Anne O'Brien of St. John's had organized a housewives' boycott of local supermarkets that was so effective the provincial government was obliged to appoint a royal commission to study the matter of food prices.

Before long, there were the Winnipeg Homemakers, the Verdun Inflation Fighters, the Ottawa Consumers' Protest Association and scores of similarly named organizations which, though unco-ordinated, mounted what in effect was a nationwide boycott of the chain food stores where most Canadians did their shopping.

Mrs. Nadine Wilson, president of the Ottawa Consumers' Protest Association, announced:

Someone in the middle – between the farmer and the supermarket – is making a tremendous profit. The boat needs to be rocked until it tips right over so we can see what comes to the top.

Chain presidents denied that the consumer boycotts of the summer and fall of 1966 had any effect on them, maintaining that supply and demand regulated food prices, including the cost of turnips. But in the wake of consumer protest, the prices seemed to pause a little before rising again.

If people power had a definable birthdate, it was probably back on July 29, 1963, in a sagging frame building called the Hall of the Rising Sun on the Garden River Ojibway Indian reserve near Sault Ste. Marie, Ontario.

At the time, Canada's 250,000 Indians lived in poverty on scattered reserves, land granted them only because it was generally too remote and barren for the white man to want for himself. The Indian infant mortality rate was ninety-seven per thousand – four times the national average. The average lifespan of an Indian woman was barely

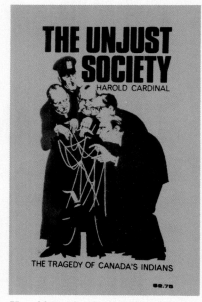

Harold Cardinal, president of the Indian Association of Alberta and a militant leader of the National Indian Brotherhood, tore into the "Just Society" campaign promises of the Trudeau government in The Unjust Society (1969), denouncing the new Indian policy as "a thinly disguised program of extermination."

NOTICE

THIS IS AN INDIAN RESERVE

Any person who trespasses on an Indian Reserve is guilty of an offence and is liable on summary conviction to a fine not exceeding fifty dollars or to imprisonment for a term not exceeding one month, or to both fine and imprisonment.

Department of Indian Affairs and Northern Development, OTTAWA.

Out of sight/out of mind for nearly a century, Indian leaders like singer Buffy Sainte-Marie, CBC's Johnny Yesno, MP Len Marchand and "Red Power" activists pointed to the relentless poverty, alcoholism and suicide rate on reserves and urged natives to stand up for their rights.

thirty.

Canada still practised its own form of segregation. There were many people like the parents in Shelley in northern British Columbia, who in 1960 fought a plan to intergrate Indian children into the local school because the Indian children would be "a moral and physical menace" to the white students.

In 1960, William Wuttunee, a Cree lawyer in Calgary, founded the National Indian Council with the aim of "helping Indians help themselves." At the third annual conference held that July on the Garden River reserve there was a confrontation between young radicals, who saw the council as a means to forge Indians into a group wielding political and economic clout, and moderates, who favoured more polite moral suasion to get a better deal from the white man.

Red Power

The radicals' voice was that of Kahn-Tineta Horn, a twenty-two-year-old Mohawk from Montreal, better known to the white world as fashion model Audrey Horn. She had earlier been Princess Kanata (Mohawk for "Canada"), the Indian Council's beauty queen. Anti-radical forces rallied around Alaise O'Bomsawin, an Abnaki also from Quebec. She was internationally known as a folk singer and was also a princess, with the Indian name, Ko-Li-La-Wato (You-have-pleased-us).

During the first sunny day of the conference, the two women stood at either side of the ninety-year-old Hall of the Rising Sun and hurled insults at one another over the heads of the delegates, mostly bemused and somewhat older chiefs. Both failed to get elected to the council executive.

The battle of the Indian princesses dramatized the issues, forced Indians to choose sides. And by the end of the decade the new sense of urgency and pride led the Indian people to try to wring a better deal from the Department of Indian Affairs. It wasn't easy. Mr. Justice J. H. Sissons, of the N.W.T.'s territorial court described the government branch as "a colonial bureaucracy swollen with its own authority that has attempted to ride roughshod over the rights and liberties of its subjects."

It was not particularly surprising that the emergence of what came to be called Red Power was led by women. Wilderness work on remote reserves was for the men, and most boys were taken out of school sooner than girls. If there was anything to be learned at school it was white man's culture – how to fight it, or at least use it.

Operation Parapluie

Less easy to explain was the 1965 rebellion known as Operation Parapluie – "umbrella" – in which the women in rural Quebec ignored their husbands and took on fledgling politician René Lévesque in what was probably his first and most frightening confrontation with the latent powers of democracy.

Midway through the 1950s, the Quebec government had installed thirty propane-powered cloud-seeding machines on the north shores of the St. Lawrence. When the wind blew from the south the generators would send a spume of silver iodide crystals into low-slung clouds to increase rainfall and so diminish the threat of inland forest fires. Local people said the system worked so well that by 1964 it rained in that area for sixty-nine of the first ninety days of spring and summer. The following year it was even wetter, and local farmers sued the provincial government for $5.3 million in crop damage. As Quebec's resources minister, René Lévesque was able to handle that problem adroitly: he had the government pay the bill. Satisfied with the settlement, the men let the matter drop. Local women were outraged.

Camped on the steps of the Manitoba Legislature, perennial protester Joe Borowski airs his beef over provincial taxes in 1966. Elected MLA in '69, he served briefly as highways' minister in Ed Schreyer's NDP government until he quit over subsidies to hospitals performing abortions.

Clouds of smoke and noxious fumes billow from a Calgary chemical plant's stacks, spread by the wind over farms, houses, reservoirs, rivers . . . By the late-60s, scientists and concerned citizens all realized that the future itself was at stake if pollution continued unchecked, but who was to pay for the clean-up?

Operation Parapluie began in the township of Alma. There, local mothers claimed that the endless rain damaged their physical and mental health and caused the bone disease called rickets as well as various respiratory and skin ailments in their children. They demanded – and got – support from four hospitals, one doctors' clinic and twenty-six municipal councils, including those of Alma, Jonquière, Chicoutimi, Roberval and Kenogami. Ten local Chambers of Commerce, three school boards, two fish and game associations and the zoo at St. Félicien also supported the protest. By the time they finished they had an anti-rainmaking petition signed by 60,718 women, declaring "the entire population of Lac St-Jean demands its place in the sun."

Confronted with an army of irate women, René Lévesque tried to placate them by distributing pastel coloured sun parasols imported from Hong Kong. The women didn't think it was funny. Next he tried to confuse the outraged women with figures which, he said, proved the rainmaking machines had no effect on the rainfall at all. That didn't work either. In the end, Lévesque and the forestry industry capitulated and dismantled the rainmakers.

The supermarket boycott, the battle of the Indian princesses and Operation Parapluie were isolated incidents. But from mid-decade on, people power became a fact of daily life.

contaminated whalemeat

The most obvious threat to the people was the way in which urban and technological wastes were damaging the environment. In this, we became an object lesson to the world. Canada made up of six per cent of the earth's land surface, endowed with twenty-five per cent of the world's fresh water and barely half a per cent of the world's population. Yet by the end of the decade, you couldn't eat the fish from almost a third of our rivers. Even Hudson's Bay was so contaminated by mercury carried down river from inland industries that in 1969 thousands of cans of Hudson's Bay whalemeat had to be destroyed because they contained mercury.

Lake Erie was the biggest shock. By 1966, an American task force of scientists ended a three-year study of the oldest and shallowest of the Great Lakes and announced that, biologically speaking, great tracts of the lakebed were "dead." Pollution – mainly from the United States – was so severe that one Ohio river that drained into the lake had actually been labelled a fire hazard because of the debris and inflammable chemicals it contained.

endangered species

Someone noticed that the peregrine falcon had disappeared from eastern North America, killed off by overdoses of chemical pesticides and fertilizers. The legendary salmon of the Miramichi River in New Brunswick had all but vanished, driven from spawning grounds by zinc and copper from a mine. In Ottawa, House of Commons windows facing the Rideau River could not be opened because of the stink of the coffee-coloured river. Along the Atlantic coast and the Bay of Fundy shoreline shellfish and lobster beds were "condemned" – that is, fishing was banned in places where even clams had absorbed so many pollutants they were inedible.

In the high Arctic, lemmings and seals and polar bears were found to have massive doses of potentially lethal chemicals in their bodies. In defiance of a 1932 court order, Montreal still poured some of its untreated sewage into the St. Lawrence River near the man-made islands that housed the 1967 world's fair. The water drawn from the St. Lawrence had to be perfumed and tinted for fear

The first organizations to arouse public awareness of the enormity of the pollution problem were often branded troublemakers and prophets of doomsday. Their message, however, was crystal clear. In the words of one Pollution Probe advertisement: "If smoking gives you lung cancer, you give up smoking, right? Now, if breathing gives you lung cancer, what are you supposed to give up?" Founded in 1969 at the University of Toronto, Pollution Probe became the model for watch-dog committees around the country, such as GASP (Group Action to Stop Pollution), sponsor of this "Clean Air" poster.

Junkyards—the landmarks of a no deposit, no return *society—speak of decades of built-in obsolescence and reckless spending. In the year 2060, would we rocket our garbage to the moon?*

Expo visitors would smell or see the truth.

Environmental groups mushroomed: GASP (Group Action to Stop Pollution); STOP (Save Tomorrow—Outlaw Pollution); and Vancouver's SPEC (Society for Pollution and Environmental Control). The most effective group was probably Ontario's Pollution Probe, which had the prestige and power of University of Toronto scientists behind it. By 1969, there were more than fifty environmental groups in Canada. They wrote letters, held meetings, staged protest marches, held symbolic funeral services for wildlife killed by pollution, and ultimately staged a requiem for the human race. High schools commonly ran projects to make students aware of pollution. In Nova Scotia, for instance, students surveyed single mile-long stretches of highway, and in one stretch picked up 1,000 candy wrappers, 350 cigarette boxes, 637 beer, pop and liquor bottles, 26 odd shoes, 30 pieces of clothing and 9 dead animals, including one horse.

Finally, the people saw their power taking effect. By 1969, the environmental groups had so dramatized the problem that a Gallup Poll found sixty-nine per cent of Canadians believed pollution was "very serious" and were even willing to pay more taxes to control it. Compelled to act by public concern, all levels of government began to review environmental laws.

hydro power or people power?

In Manitoba, the Conservative government was defeated partly because it supported plans to flood two Indian settlements and a massive area of land around Southern Indian Lake for a hydro electric power development. Because of native people's and conservationists protests, the hydro development had become a critical campaign issue.

In cities rent battles toward the end of the dec-

106

ade were enough to alert governments to the need for some controls. Throughout the decade cities climbed skyward until almost half the nation's population lived in highrise apartments and other rental accommodation. After 1966, accommodation became scarce and property owners tried to profit from the situation. In Winnipeg in 1966, a landlord opened a new building and, to fill it quickly, offered the apartments at low rents. When, in 1968, the leases came up for renewal, he jacked up the rents thirty per cent. It was a legal tactic under landlord and tenant laws on all provincial statute books. The tenants formed what amounted to a rate payers' group, and refused to pay. They won their battle and that encouraged the founding of the Canadian Tenants' Association.

cancelled taxes

Winnipeg was following trends set in Vancouver. There one landlord said a $10-a-month rent hike was due to a tax increase. One tenant did some homework and proved the tax raise amounted to forty-three cents per suite. In the upper-class Montreal suburb of Outremont, the town council slapped a "temporary" seven per cent tax on the borough's five thousand tenants, who promptly formed an association, marched on city hall and forced the cancellation of the tax.

The case of the people *versus* development was an even better example of the way protest changed things in the sixties. Toronto embarked on an urban renewal scheme in a rundown area known as Don Mount. More than two hundred single-family homes were expropriated and demolished, their owners accepting whatever the city offered them. One elderly woman refused to sell. Dorothy Graham argued that the market value of her home was irrelevant; what mattered was how much it would cost her to buy another one. Stubbornly, she sat in

The Star Forum takes a hard look at the cold war between landlords and tenants.

Right now, Queen's Park is studying 24 proposed revisions to Ontario's archaic Landlord and Tenants Act, which places grotesquely one-sided powers in the hands of landlords. The abuses permitted by the Act have divided landlords and tenants into warring camps. To the majority of the more than 600,000 apartment dwellers in Metro Toronto, soaring rents, restrictive leases and high security deposits are problems of urgent concern. What can be done about them?

On Thursday, May 15, in this newspaper, The Star Forum with Editor-in-Chief Peter C. Newman as moderator, will present a comprehensive report on landlord-tenant relations, with specific proposals for reform in the drawing up of leases.

What is The Star Forum? To keep its readers informed on questions of vital public concern, The Toronto Daily Star has established a new department — The Star Forum — with The Star's Editor-in-Chief Peter C. Newman as moderator. The Star Forum will focus on problems of the day, bring together panels of experts to discuss them, conduct surveys and investigations — and report the results to readers. In this presentation, The Star Forum will publish an account of a panel discussion between landlords and tenants. Rent controls, security deposits, simplified leases, right of entry, rent review boards and rent strikes are some of the controversial issues which will be covered in detail by informed, articulate representatives of both groups. An important feature of this extensive, interesting report in Thursday's Daily Star will be a Star Forum manifesto on methods of achieving a new deal for tenants and landlords through revisions to Ontario's Landlords and Tenants Act. Don't miss this Star Forum report on Thursday, May 15.

The first.
Toronto Daily Star

Ad hoc *groups who got and kept their gripes on TV and in the papers found that boycotts, class-action law suits, picketing, ads,* whatever . . . *accomplished more than letters to* MPs *and* MPPs.

STOP AMCHITKA STOP THE WAR

Sat. Nov. 6 - Ontario Demonstration
Assemble North End of Queens Park, Toronto 2pm

Stop Amchitka Bomb Test
End Canada's Complicity in U.S. War Machine
Withdraw All U.S. Troops from Vietnam Now

Vietnam Mobilization Committee
241 Victoria St. Toronto 863-0494

As though the ghosts of Hiroshima and Nagasaki were not evidence enough of this awesome power, on October 2, 1969, the United States (just testing) exploded a one megaton nuclear bomb on Amchitka, one of the Aleutian Islands off Alaska. Canada, Japan, the Soviet Union and other nations protested in the name of good sense: Alaska had just been shaken by a major earthquake; this blast could shake up another. Vancouver's Don't Make A Wave Committee (the forerunner of Greenpeace) tried to "make waves" in the test zone but was snafu'd. What the exercise produced (besides radiation) remains a Pentagon "Top Secret."

her house as the neighbourhood was demolished and foundation pits for new buildings were dug. Finally the city capitulated. The "house for a house" principle became part of municipal expropriation in Toronto, for a while.

In 1968, the people of Trefann Court, an area of about four blocks in Toronto, also refused to go quietly. Confronted with city ordinances to abandon their homes to the bulldozers, the people of Trefann Court formed an association; found an energetic young lawyer to be their spokesman; mounted what by now was a familiar campaign of negotiating with the council on the one hand, and gaining publicity and public sympathy on the other. Ultimately the people of Trefann Court won.

the bulldozers are coming

Shirley Chan was a twenty-one-year-old university student who lived with her family in Strathcona, part of Vancouver's Chinatown. Since 1958, the area had been under a death sentence because the city had approved a redevelopment project similar to Trefann Court. As a result, the five hundred houses awaiting demolition had become rundown: why paint the porch when the bulldozer was coming? In 1968, Shirley Chan, a forceful young woman, went to war on behalf of the residents. She didn't want to swap her home for a unit in a highrise beehive. She founded the Strathcona Property Owners' and Tenants' Association, and finally persuaded the federal government to withdraw the $2 million it had promised to contribute to the development. More important, after hearing the association's arguments, the Liberal minister then responsible for housing, Robert Andras, told city politicians that local residents must in future always be involved in development for which the

federal government was helping to pay.

People power was collective action. Even in 1962 it had become apparent that the individual should not stand alone against big government and big business. That year the Royal Commission on Government Organization reported that the federal civil service was far bigger than it need be and that a large slice of it should be dismantled. By mid-decade there were demands that governments appoint ombudsmen to protect the people from the bureaucracies that were set up to serve them.

"champions of the little man"

In the absence of government action, newspapers appointed their own ombudsmen. In May 1966, the Toronto *Telegram* started a column called "Action Line," which immediately found itself dealing with one or two *thousand* problems a week. Soon afterward, newspapers in Vancouver, Ottawa, London, Montreal and other cities appointed their own "champions of the little man." Significantly, as the decade ended half the complaints they handled involved computers, which had by then already taken over a large part of business, goverment and private life.

People and computers seemed increasingly incompatible. One much cited case handled by the Toronto *Telegram's* Frank Drea involved a woman who had ordered one five-pound bag of Kitty Litter from a department store catalogue computer. The system proceeded to hiccough the order out *day after day* until soon she had 250 pounds of the stuff stacked on her front porch. She told Drea: "I've called the store, but it still keeps coming, and kitty is wondering how to live up to the computer's expectations. Those machines don't understand about cats, either."

Ecologists warned that it was only a matter of time before this disaster, resulting from the collision of two boats in Vancouver's Narrows, would occur again, coating Atlantic or Pacific beaches with crude oil. Would it be Chedabucto Bay, near the supertanker docks at Port Hawkesbury, Nova Scotia?

Qu'est-ce que vous me chantez?

Qu'est-ce que vous me chantez? The question doesn't mean "What's the name of that song?" but "What kind of line are you handing me?" What was the the "line" these *chansonniers* were singing? Quite simply, a free and independent Quebec. The idea ran through Vigneault's Poetic *"Mon Pays,"* Leclerc's biting *"Les Mauvais Conseils,"* Charlebois' satirical "Frog Song." Below (clockwise from the top) Robert Charlebois, Claude Léveillée, Gilles Vigneault, Yvon Deschamps, Jean-Pierre Ferland.

CHAPTER TEN

The Unquiet Revolution

For Quebec today the choice is not between two systems more or less favourable to its overall progress. The choice is simply one between a good life and a slow death. And we cannot play hide-and-seek with history by saying, "We aren't ready yet . . ."

René Lévesque, *An Option for Quebec,* 1968

Most of English Canada couldn't understand what the fuss was about, but to French Canadians it seemed inevitable that the decade should end in violence. And it was fitting that in 1968 the manifesto of the age and rage of French Canada's youth should be a book in which Pierre Vallières described Quebeckers in the title as *White Niggers of America:* Canada's "cheap labour that the predators of industry, commerce and high finance are so fond of, the way wolves are fond of sheep."

Paradoxically, to the rest of the nation it seemed that French Canadians had more reason for dissatisfaction when the decade began than when it ended. Though premier Maurice Duplessis had died in 1959, his Union Nationale government continued to keep itself in power with a patronage system that, when he investigated it later, Mr. Justice Elie Salvas described as an "immoral, scandalous, humiliating and alarming system of graft and kickbacks." Even the suppliers of paint for white lines on highways paid bribes.

Most rural Quebeckers were poor. Worst off were farmers in the far reaches of the province– Lake St. John, Abitibi, along the lower St. Lawrence and the Gaspé regions. Far from their markets, they fought depleted soil and bad climate and, as late as the middle of the decade, they cleared an annual income of only $1200. Many farm boys migrated to the city, but things were no rosier there. Early in the decade, fully a third of the population of Montreal was so poor they couldn't buy more than their daily necessities.

Jobs were scarce everywhere. Even those lucky enough to find a job often found that they were underpaid. Average wages in Quebec were well below wages in other provinces, a fact which prompted labour leader Louis Laberge to demand: "Give me a good reason why the workers at Ste-Thérèse earn 50 to 60 cents an hour less than those at Ottawa or Windsor. Our cars aren't any cheaper just because our men are paid less."

In 1960, the church still dominated small-town society, and nowhere was this more apparent than in education. It was the job of the Church to raise the future generations and schools were run by a Council of Public Instruction made up of clergy. Educational structures were so confused that if an orphan's father had been a farmer, his or her education was the responsibility of the provincial department of agriculture. High schools charged for both tuition and textbooks. Students from large

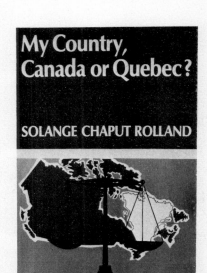

One Quebec journalist in search of a country, Solange Chaput Rolland crossed Canada in 1966, asking herself and others this question. She sadly admitted her answer: Quebec.

Opposite page: *Montreal's "finest" had ample opportunity to try out their new riot gear and mob-control tactics, but when firemen and the cops themselves went out on strike on October 7, 1969, the army had to be called in to quell rioters, looters and vandals in the city.*

Angered by the appointment of an American director, nationalists tore down Place des Arts banners during the opening concert at Montreal's $9-million Salle Wilfred Pelletier in fall 1963.

families and poor areas rarely got an education that equipped them to get out of the farmlands. Elsewhere in Canada the school-leaving age was sixteen; in Quebec it was still fourteen, and that's when most kids quit.

In 1960, French Canada produced only ten per cent of the country's doctors and an even smaller proportion of its dentists, accountants, professors, engineers and scientists. Donald Gordon, then president of Canadian National Railways, said bluntly that the reason there were so few French Canadians in CN's top management was that so few of them qualified by education for the jobs. For saying that, Gordon was burned in effigy during a Montreal rally that became a near riot.

But after the death of Duplessis the critics from within Quebec society began to be heard, and they were heeded.

Parles-tu joual?

In 1960, Jean-Paul Desbiens, a thirty-three-year-old teaching brother of the Marist Order in Montreal, wrote *Les Insolences du frère Untel*. In the book he said French Canada's language was *joual* – his spelling of the manner in which most Quebeckers pronounced the word *cheval*, a horse. "One speaks *joual* so one lives *joual* and thinks *joual*" he wrote. "Our inability to assert ourselves, our rejection of the future and our obsession with the past is reflected in *joual*, which is truly our language."

The book sold a staggering 127,000 copies in six months. For writing it Desbiens was banished to Rome and later to Switzerland. But the book's impact, however, meant that an intellectual like Pierre Elliott Trudeau was taken seriously when he said: "It is a waste of time for our politicians to spit on the English. It's not the fault of the English that we're a backward province. We're responsible for our own mess."

114

That a new vitality was sweeping away the old Duplessis policy of *survivance* – mere survival in an alien culture – became apparent during the campaign that led to the provincial election of June 22, 1960. The opposition Liberals had an energetic new leader, Jean Lesage, who had attracted a formidable array of candidates, including René Lévesque, a journalist and radical who had become one of the new breed of celebrities created by the CBC's French television network. The Liberals launched an all-out attack on the Union Nationale and the corruption it represented.

$25 a vote

The election that summer was typical of the way things had been. Journalist Catherine Breslin, then living in Montreal, voted twenty times, being paid $25 a vote by the Union Nationale which provided her with false identities. Montreal police reported seventy-one ballot boxes stolen from polling stations; four campaign workers who needed hospital treatment for injuries suffered in brawls outside voting booths; and 158 arrests made in raids on party committee rooms.

Even so, Lesage's Liberals won fifty-one seats and, with a majority of six, took power. Duplessis had tried to preserve Quebec as a French enclave in English North America by shutting out the rest of the world. Lesage and his lieutenants, René Lévesque and Paul Gérin-Lajoie, set out to drag the province into equal partnership with *les anglais*, while promoting what they called "Québecitude."

Everything seemed to happen at once. There was revolution in the church, schools, universitites, government and the arts. And Jean Lesage was a symbol of the new Quebec. In 1960, he was forty-eight, a distinguished, autocratic and incorruptible man who abandoned his federal cabinet post and a career in federal politics to devote his energies to

July 25, 1963

"Royal commission or no royal commission, I'll thank you to keep the English side of the box pointing my way . . ."

March 23, 1963

"I say let Quebec secede . . . Ottawa might then be jolly well glad to ask us to join Canada."

Westerners who groused about bilingual flacons de maïs *boxes and separatism bristled when B.C. loaned Quebec $100 million (a third of U.S. payments in 1964 for Columbia power) for Expo.*

The little book that rocked Quebec, Les Insolences du Frère Untel *by Jean-Paul Desbiens, soared to the top of the bestseller list in the wake of the "Quiet Revolution." Its author, a 33-year-old Marist Brother, criticized both the Roman Catholic Church and the education system for the cultural feudalism of the province.* Joual, the dialect of the man in the street, reflected the lack of pride and assertiveness that had kept the province on its knees, he explained. Forced to do "penance" in Switzerland for his impertinence (the Church had not seen or approved the book before publication), he returned to a new, vitalized Quebec in 1965, where he was given a post in the totally-revamped Department of Education.

Quebec. He was the catalyst of the "Quiet Revolution" through which Quebec began to throw off the bonds of religious and social conformity and set out to determine its own fate.

It soon became apparent, however, that Lesage's radical conscience was René Lévesque, the minister of resources who set about taking over privately-owned power stations to create a province-owned electrical utility.

Angavorkra

Power was vital to Quebec's industrial future, and Lévesque saw that only a big public company could ultimately provide that power and employ Quebeckers to build and operate it. One of the motives of Hydro Quebec was to provide jobs in construction and management for Quebeckers. Many of the power-station developments he initiated were in the north, where the Inuit came to call him *Angavorkra*, or Great White Chief.

Lévesque was unassuming to the point of self-effacement. He said: "I'm a normally intelligent guy, and if I have any qualifications for my present job it's that I have no real interest in money or big friends with money."

One inevitable consequence of this new national pride was resentment by French Canadians who still had to learn English to work. Because Quebec had not provided enough engineers and managers, the mines and hydro construction projects were still run by *les anglais*. In 1964, more than half the French Canadians in Montreal were fluently bilingual, but only five per cent of English Canadian Montrealers could manage more than *bonjour*.

Elsewhere, Canada wasn't at all bilingual. In 1966, Ralph Cowan, a Liberal MP from Toronto, received almost a thousand approving letters from English Canadians after telling a students' rally at Jonquière in Quebec: "It's time you all accepted the English conquest of 1763, just as the English accepted conquest by William the Conqueror." French Canada didn't like Ralph Cowan. Nor was French Canada happy when *La Presse* sent reporter Jean Rivest to Toronto for a weekend and he reported:

In one day because I couldn't speak English I couldn't buy an airplane ticket, I caused a panic in the Royal York, practically disorganized Bell Telephone's long distance system and could not even get directions around the city.

Given these attitudes elsewhere in Canada, it was inevitable that in a newly liberated society impatient men would propose revolutionary changes. In 1961 three separatist organizations were formed. There was the right wing *Alliance Laurentienne* which claimed two thousand members; the left wing *Action Socialiste pour l'Indépendance du Québec*; and the moderate and ultimately more durable *Rassemblement pour l'Indépendance Nationale*.

Why I Am A Separatist

By far the best known was the latter, the RIN, founded as a movement to educate Quebeckers about independence. One of its early presidents, federal government scientist Marcel Chaput, argued that separatism was a "serious and credible" option for Quebec. Chaput pushed separatism as the only way to restore his dream of "French dignity in the new world."

In his 1961 book entitled *Pourquoi je suis séparatiste*, Chaput affirmed:

I am a Canadian, and as long as Canada remains what it is, I shall remain loyal to Canada and the Queen. But as a free man and a French Canadian, I believe that I have the right to question the political institutions of this country and to express the wish that French Canada soon be relieved of her allegiance to the British Crown.

Sergeant-Major Walter Leja lies in the gutter, critically wounded by the explosion of a mailbox bomb he was attempting to dismantle. It was one of four bombs found in Montreal's English-speaking Westmount that day — May 17, 1963. A month before, a night watchman had been killed by a similar bomb.

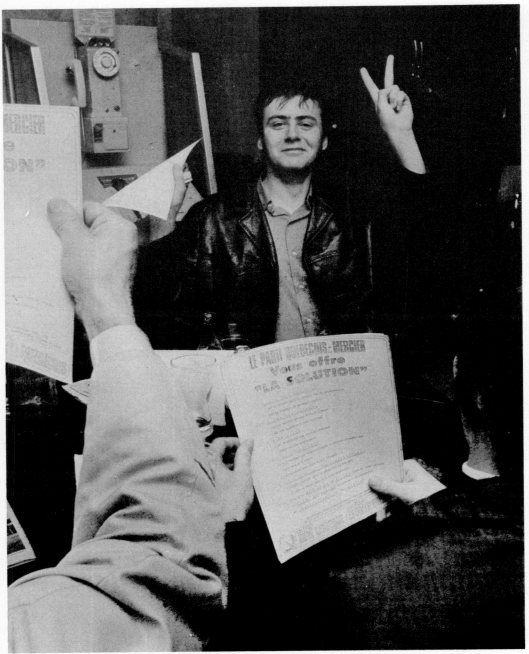

Formed in October 1968, the Parti Québécois under René Lévesque went to the voters with a clear-cut separatist platform, "La Solution," in April 1970, and won 24% of the popular vote.

When the government suspended him without pay for attending a separatist conference in 1961, Chaput resigned vowing never to use the English language again.

Later separatist leaders would remember Chaput as the dreamer, and the RIN as "timid." That same year, 1961, separatists tore down a Union Jack flying outside the Sherbrooke headquarters of the Canadian Legion, and later painted the words "traitor" and "liberty" on the home of a former commander of the famous Vingt-deuxième (Van Doos) Régiment.

In November 1961, Laval University in Quebec City held a top-level conference on the subject: "The Canadian Experiment: Success or Failure." One speaker pointed out:

A French-Canadian taxpayer who writes in his own language to a federal department will usually find that his letter is sent to the translating system before reaching the official concerned, even if the official is French. And the reply will follow the same course.

Meanwhile René Lévesque said that he was still a Canadian federalist, but warned the other nine provinces: "You need us more than we need you."

When Jean Lesage went to the people in 1962, he campaigned with the slogan: *Maîtres chez nous* – Masters in Our Own House. He was not a separatist, he said; he was French Canadian, but spoke for a people who wanted more control over their own affairs than Ottawa seemed prepared to give them. Lesage won the big majority he wanted and for a few months it seemed like a triumph of reason over revolution.

cocktails at midnight

The first bomb was a Molotov cocktail – a bottle filled with gasoline, its neck stuffed with a burning rag. One night in March 1963, it was tossed against the wall of a wooden Canadian National

Railways building in midtown Montreal. *Vive le Québec libre* was scrawled on a nearby wall. That phrase would become one of the most chilling slogans in Canadian history.

That first bomb had been heralded by letters to Montreal newspapers announcing the creation of the *Front de Libération du Québec*, which consisted of groups of "suicide commandos" whose job was "to destroy completely by systematic sabotage all the symbols of colonial institutions."

A few more fire bombs were dumped near armouries, and later that spring dynamite bombs were found and dismantled in the Montreal head post office in Place Ville-Marie, and in an air vent of the National Revenue Building. A lighted stick of dynamite blew up when thrown against the wall of RCMP divisional headquarters.

the "Quiet Revolution" ends

Even so, the "Quiet Revolution" did not become lethal until late that April. In the army recruiting centre across the street from McGill University's front gate, there was an explosion that killed an elderly night watchman, Wilfrid O'Neill. Montreal police formally admitted that urban terrorism, the weapon of guerillas and rebel factions for decades throughout the world, was now a fact of life in Canada.

Later that month the FLQ invaded Westmount, the Montreal district where most of the English-speaking elite of Quebec lived. At 3:11 A.M. one Friday morning, a dynamite bomb blew up in a mailbox outside St. Mathias Anglican Church, splintering the church door and breaking sixteen nearby windows. Between then and 3:30 A.M., four more mailboxes blew up. Army demolition experts checked every one of the eighty-five remaining Westmount mailboxes. They found four more bombs. Three they dismantled safely, the fourth blew up, maiming the bomb-disposal expert. Next

Mayor Jean Drapeau (who brought you Expo, the Expos and the Vaisseau d'Or restaurant) is the chef behind separatist cartoonist Dupras' mock-recipe for a perfect Montreal omelette.

Had the times been different, the now-famous remarks of Charles de Gaulle in Montreal might have gone down as the last power-and-glory speech of a tired, old general. As Le Devoir editor Claude Ryan said, "The worst error English Canadians can commit would be to remember only the words 'Long live a free Quebec' and to forget the rest . . .," the need for Canada to settle its own problems without interference.

morning, police on Montreal island formed a two-hundred-man special squad and declared "total war on terrorists."

On June 17, police arrested seventeen college-age terrorists. Canadians reassured themselves by calling them the "lunatic fringe." Fifteen of those arrested were eventually jailed – the Belgian-born ringleader, Georges Schoeters, for ten years. Montreal police chief J. Adrien Robert called a press conference to announce that the FLQ was smashed, broke, a spent force.

One chill morning the next January, the night watchman at the *Fusiliers de Montréal* armouries in east-end Montreal opened the door at 7:35 a.m. to a gang of teenagers flourishing sawed-off shotguns and a pistol. They tied him up and drove off in an army truck loaded with 30 sten guns, 2 machine guns, 4 mortars, 59 semi-automatic rifles, 11 walkie-talkies and 17,266 rounds of ammunition.

They did it again and again in the next few weeks, and RCMP Deputy Commissioner J. R. Lemieux eventually said enough arms had been stolen in armoury raids "to start a small war." The robbers claimed to be part of the *Mouvement Révolutionnaire du Québec.*

"the wild man of Quebec"

René Lévesque, by now described by some English journalists as "the wild man of Quebec," said publicly: "Look, whatever you call me, I am in fact nothing more than a forty-year-old moderate. There are young guys behind me who make me feel nervous."

At successive provincial constitutional conferences during the 1960s, Quebec continued to press for greater provincial autonomy, and Ottawa handed over more and more responsibilities to the provinces, along with the money to meet them. Quebec opted out of several federal-provincial programmes – the Canada Pension Plan, for one –

but did receive its share of the federal funds earmarked for the schools. As one civil servant summed up a 1964 federal-provincial conference: "It's finally sinking in that all the premiers want central Canada to be strong. On the other hand, Quebec is fundamentally opposed to the idea of a strong central government."

Chatty Cathy

Ottawa tried to quiet Quebec in other ways, too. When the decade began, the French wording on a package of corn flakes occupied a quarter of the back of the package. By the mid-sixties, it occupied the entire back of the package, a change ordered as part of the growing federal programme of bilingualism. Canadian National Railways announced that it would have its name in both English and French painted on all its 100,000 boxcars. That meant having "Canadien National" as well as "Canadian National" on the railcars, a paint job that involved only one letter in the name and was then estimated to take thirteen years. The big thing with little girls in 1965 was a talking doll called Chatty Cathy. She was bilingual.

In the spring of 1966, Jean Lesage called his third election in six years, saying he needed a strong mandate to take a tough line with English Canada. Pundits everywhere assumed he would emerge with an even larger majority in a legislature that now had 107 seats. Again, Lesage made a valiant pitch to the farmers. There would be harvest insurance, he said, and bad weather indemnities and soil replacement programmes.

But some traditions die hard. The rural farmers had kept Duplessis in power, and Duplessis had reciprocated with local favours: a new road, for example, if the candidate won. It was all very well for the Liberals to attack the shameful practice of patronage, but in 1966 one of the Liberal candidates still received the following letter:

One columnist noted the absence of the Canadian flag en route. Most noticed the boos and hisses when "God Save The Queen" (indeed) was played. But no one, including the most ardent separatists, realized what impact French President Charles de Gaulle's visit in July 1967 would have on Canada's 100th birthday.

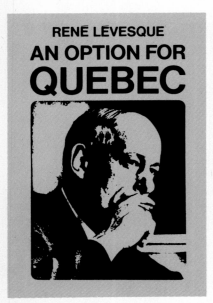

**RENÉ LÉVESQUE
AN OPTION FOR
QUEBEC**

In two short years of leadership at the helm of the independence movement in Quebec, René Lévesque turned around the "lost cause" of separatism from an "Option" to a "Solution" (see page 118). To a few English Canadians it seemed a bit strange: a federalist prime minister (Pierre Trudeau, once a confrère of Lévesque) trying to keep the nation together; while another French Canadian was doing his best to tear the country apart.

Opposite page: *John Diefenbaker was the first to call them "The Three Wise Men" when they first made their journey to Ottawa in 1965, to take up jobs in a government dominated by well-meaning, English-speaking Liberals. Jean Marchand, Pierre Trudeau, Gérard Pelletier: would they be the "Wise Men" who kept Canada together?*

We want to move our house and we want to know if you can help us buy the cement for the new foundation. We would like a grant and that is why we are writing to you. If you want to have our vote on June 5, please answer before the elections. Otherwise, we won't vote.

And so Lesage found that this time the farmers weren't buying. Rural Quebec, which knew about the "Quiet Revolution" mainly because it had to foot its own bills, swept Daniel Johnson's Union Nationale party into power. The political soothsayers, backtracking, now claimed the victory was due to the feeling in rural Quebec that the revolution had gone too far too fast.

"Vive le Québec libre!"

Centennial year came, and with it French president Charles de Gaulle's visit to Expo, during which he waved to crowds from the balcony of Montreal City Hall, and shouted *"Vive le Québec! Vive le Québec libre! Vive le Canada français! Vive la France!"* Scarcely three months later, at a Liberal party congress, René Lévesque officially declared his belief in separatism and broke with the Liberals to form the *Mouvement Souveraineté-Association*. The effervescent Lévesque galvanized separatist sentiment, and within a year, two other separatist organizations joined with Lévesque's MSA to form the *Parti Québécois*.

Still, when Montreal hosted the highlight of the national birthday party, there seemed to be less urgency in Prime Minister Lester Pearson's study of how the rest of Canada would fare in the event of Quebec's secession. In fact, tension eased on the subject of bilingualism, despite the fact that in its interim report in 1965, the Royal Commission on Bilingualism and Biculturalism had reported: "We

have found evidence of serious danger to the continued existence of Canada."

By 1968, there was a new prime minister in Ottawa, burdened with the task of keeping the improbable entity called Canada together. Pierre Elliott Trudeau had proclaimed his dream of a "just society," and the first major piece of this new society's legislation was the Official Languages Act. It stated that, as a matter of national principle, all Canadians should be able to deal with the federal government and courts in either French or English, wherever ten per cent of the local population claimed either French or English as its native tongue. Most Canadians accepted the new PM and the legislation with pride and optimism.

futile efforts?

The Act was passed, but to the separatists of Quebec it meant nothing. By mid-1968 the bombs were exploding again, and all of Trudeau's efforts seemed futile. By March 1969, there had been sixty-four bombings of armouries, public buildings and premises of firms considered "colonial."

That year a visiting reporter sat in the Canadian Legion bar in the mountain town of Hope, British Columbia, watching a game between the Montreal Canadiens and the Chicago Black Hawks on television. He asked why legion members were rooting for the American team, not the Canadian one. "There's not much liking for the Frenchies around here," he was told. "They're never satisfied with anything."

In Montreal René Lévesque, the small, slender, chain-smoking ex-Liberal sat at the head of what was clearly a vital and efficient political organization girding itself for its first election the following year. It was called the *Parti Québécois*, and its platform was built on one basic policy: Separatism.

Acknowledgements

For the author of any book on the 1960s there are no "authorities" to thank because it's all too recent, too traumatic still, for there to be handy reference books and "acknowledged experts." To find the 1960s you have to go looking the hard way, in newspaper and magazine files and in the rummage bag of memory.

For all that, I own that the work of the following people was of particular help: the editors of *Georgia Straight*, Ian Adams, Doris Anderson, Pat Annesley, Pierre Berton, June Callwood, Gordon Donaldson, Robert Fulford, Peter Gzowski, Douglas Marshall, Peter Newman, Alexander Ross, Jon Ruddy, Nicholas Steed, Borden Spears and the numberless other reporters of the social scene who at least tried to tell it the way it was while it was actually happening.

And I owe many others thanks, particularly Margaret Wente, Barbara Holmes and Clare McKeon, for re-living with me the optimism of the 1960s, a saddening process in the light of all the promises not kept, the dreams not realized.

Alan Edmonds

Photo: John Edmonds

The Author

Alan Edmonds was born in London, England, and began his career in journalism writing for weekly newspapers, the London *Daily Express* and the Manchester *Guardian*. In 1960, he came to Canada and since then has worked for the Toronto *Star*, *Maclean's*, the Toronto *Sun* and *The Canadian* magazine, with stints through Europe, the Middle East and Far East for the *Star* and the *Herald Tribune* as a roving correspondent. As writer, producer and host of television news specials and public affairs programmes, his name and face are familiar to TV viewers across Canada. Author of several books, among them *Voyage to the Edge of the World* (the account of the historic journey of the U.S. tanker *Manhattan* and the icebreaker *John A. Macdonald* through the North West Passage) and *The Ion Effect*, with his colleagues he jokes freely about the many books he has "ghosted."

Index

The page numbers in italics refer to illustrations and captions.

Picture Credits

"I miss the Fifties."

We would like to acknowledge the help and cooperation of the directors and staff of the various public institutions and the private firms and individuals who made available paintings, posters, mementos, collections and albums as well as photographs and gave us permission to reproduce them. Every effort has been made to identify and credit appropriately the sources of all illustrations used in this book. Any further information will be appreciated and acknowledged in subsequent editions.

The illustrations are listed in the order of their appearance on the page, left to right, top to bottom. Principal sources are credited under these abbreviations:

CW   Canada Wide
PAC   Public Archives of Canada
PC   Private Collection

/1 Joyce Wieland-Isaacs Gallery /2 Alex Colville /4 Canadian Opera Company /6 John de Visser /7 New American Library, Inc /8 John Max /9 CW-A. Leishman /10 Canadian Pacific /11 Toronto Star Syndicate /12 NFB Photothèque-André Sima (66-4810) /13 McClelland and Stewart /14 *Canadian Dimension* /15 John de Visser /16 Calgary *Albertan; Vancouver Sun* /17 Toronto Sun Syndicate /18 *Globe & Mail* /19 Gestetner (Canada) Ltd. /20 Duke Photo, Banff /21 Estate of William Kurelek /22 *Georgia Straight; Octopus; Harbinger Publishing* /23 *Georgia Straight; Logos; Octopus; Harbinger Publishing; Omphalos; Tribal Village* /24 Natoma Productions /25 McClelland and Stewart /26 Les Nirenberg /27 CFTO-TV, Toronto /28 CHUM, Toronto; *Vancouver Sun* /29 NFB Photothèque-Ronald Labelle (68-3866); United Church Press /30 Toronto Star Syndicate /31 John Phillips /32 Maclean-Hunter Ltée /33 Donald Van Buren-23 Skidoo /34 Capital Records-EMI of Canada, Ltd; WEA Music of Canada Ltd; London Records of Canada, Ltd /35 CBS Records Canada, Ltd; Capitol Records-EMI of Canada Ltd; United Artists Records, Ltd; WEA Music of Canada, Ltd /36 Allan King-Saturday Plays, Ltd; Cinepix, Inc. /37 Peerless Films Ltd /38 Sam Tata /39 Henri Rossier /40 Popular Library Inc; Dell Publishing Co., Inc; Popular Library, Inc; Popular Library Inc; Bantam Books, Inc; Avon Books /41 Dell Publishing Co., Inc; Bantam Books, Inc; Bantam Books, Inc. /42 Continental Films, Ltd. /43 Eaton's (67212-252) /44 Ted Herriott Associates /45 *Montreal Star*-CW /46

Arts Canada Magazine; *Arts Canada* Magazine /47 Claude Breeze-National Gallery of Canada; Michael Snow-Isaacs Gallery /48 Dennis Burton-Robert McLaughlin Gallery, Oshawa /49 Charlottetown Festival /50 Shaw Festival /51 Toronto Star Syndicate /52 National Film Board (S6850) /53 National Film Board (S2993) /54 London *Free Press* /55 CBC /56 PAC C15160 /57 PC /58 Progressive Conservative Party of Canada; Progressive Conservative Party of Canada /59 Maclean-Hunter Publishing Company; McClelland and Stewart /60 Toronto Star Syndicate /61 Bank of Nova Scotia /62 Alberta Government Publicity Bureau /63 Sid Barron /64 Bantam Books, Inc. /65 Maclean-Hunter Publishing Company /66 McClelland and Stewart /68 Ken Elliott /69 Shirley Van Buren /70 Hamilton *Spectator* /71 Halifax *Chronicle-Herald* /72 PAC 10344 /73 Toronto Star Syndicate /74 Obrazove Zpravodajstvi /75 Centennial Commission /76 PAC-3419 /77 Toronto Star Syndicate /78 Ken Elliott /79 Gordon Rayner /80 Ontario Department of Education /81 *Octopus*-Christopher Lea /82 Bill Brooks /83 Bill Brooks /84 *The Varsity*; NFB Photothèque-Mike West (66-11946) /85 Toronto Board of Education-Michael Semak; Educational Technology /86 *Globe & Mail* /87 *Octopus* /88 Corporation des Ensignants du Québec /89 Ken Elliott /90 *Canadian* Magazine-Jorgen Halling; *Canadian* Magazine-Jorgen Halling; *Canadian* Magazine-Jorgen Halling /91 *Canadian* Magazine-Jorgen Halling; *Canadian* Magazine-Jorgen Halling /92 Eberhard Otto-Miller Services /93 N.S.L. /94 NFB Photothèque-G. Lunney (64-5413) /95 Belmont Property Management /96 *Vancouver Sun* /97 Canadian Brotherhood of Railway Transport and General Workers /98 Toronto Star Syndicate /99 *Globe & Mail* /100 *Globe & Mail* /101 Hurtig Publishers /102 Department of Indian Affairs and Northern Development /103 Maclean-Hunter /104 Calgary *Herald*-Ken Sakamoto /105 Group Action To Stop Pollution /106 Ontario Department of Transportation and Communications /107 Toronto Star Syndicate /108 Vietnam Mobilization Committee /109 *Vancouver Sun* /110 Kebec Disques /111 CBS Records of Canada, Ltd; Les Disques Gamma Ltée; Polydor Ltée; Les Disques Gamma Ltée. /112 Ken Elliott /113 Macmillan of Canada /114 *Montreal Gazette* /115 *Vancouver Sun* /116 Les Editions de Homme /117 *Montreal Gazette* /118 M.G. Communications Visuelles, Inc. /119 Les Editions Québécoises; Les Editions Québécoises /121 *Montreal Star*-CW /122 McClelland & Stewart /123 PAC C25003 /128 Maclean-Hunter

128

1965

Montreal's *La Presse* presses roll after seven-month strike; Toronto's nine-month newspaper strike ends.

PM Pearson and President Johnson sign Canada-U.S. auto-pact.

Michelle Duclos of Montreal and three Americans convicted in plot to blow up Statue of Liberty.

TCA becomes Air Canada.

Petra Burka of Toronto wins women's title at World's Figure Skating Championships at Colorado Springs.

Drug smuggler Lucien Rivard escapes from Montreal's Bordeaux Prison.

Four die in accident at pirates' "money pit" on Oak Island, N.S.

CP airliner crashes on Vancouver to Prince George flight: 52 dead.

Green garbage bags come into use.

Atlantic Acceptance Corp. declares bankruptcy, owing $115 million.

a perfectly SOUND reason for LISTENING to CBC RADIO

RICH LITTLE—ONE OF THE MANY STARS OF CBC SHOWCASE

Fowler Report on broadcasting urges increased Canadian content.

George and Viola Macmillan charged with fraud in multi-million dollar Windfall Oil and Mines scandal.

Abraham Okpik becomes first Eskimo to sit on N.W.T. council.

Pearson's Liberal minority returned in November federal election.

Circuit failure at Queenston, Ont., hydro station blacks out entire northeastern U.S. and Canada.

Paris designers shock the fashion world with the mini-skirt.

1966

Vancouver postal clerk Victor Spencer fired for part in Soviet espionage plot.

Canada Pension Plan goes into effect.

Anti-Vietnam War demonstrators converge on Ottawa; 40 arrested.

Spence Commission appointed to probe Gerda Munsinger Affair.

CBC fires Patrick Watson, Laurier LaPierre and nine others over controversial "Seven Days" show.

Parent Commission report recommends revamp of Quebec school system.

Paul-Joseph Chartier killed by own bomb in Commons washroom.

Daniel Johnson leads Union Nationale to victory over Lesage Liberals in Quebec elections.

Dave Bailey of Toronto becomes first Canadian to break four-minute mile.

Divers recovers $700,000 in gold from 1725 *Chambeau* wreck off N.S.

NHL announces six-team expansion.

Marie-Claire Blais wins Prix Medicis for *Une Saison dans la Vie d'Emmanuel*.

Eight arrested in $3 million heroin "bust" in Montreal.

Ottawa housewives spark nation-wide supermarket boycott over prices.

cbc's new dimension

In Color

CBC-TV

CBC-TV begins telecasting in "living colour."

Brian Parks of Winnipeg wins World Bridge Trophy.

PAINT COMPLETELY TOPLESS GIRLS
"NO PASTIES"
Also Nude Movies from Europe
114 YORKVILLE
MON.-SAT.
8:30 p.m.-2:30 a.m.
RESERVATIONS
922-5404
THE MYNAH BIRD

The Cat's Whiskers, Canada's first "topless" bar, opens in Vancouver.

Montreal's Métro (subway) opens.

Saskatchewan beats Ottawa 29-14 for Grey Cup after night of revelry and riots in Vancouver.

1967

Happy Centennial! Let's have a wonderful year. 1867 | 1967

Prime Minister Pearson lights Centennial Flame on Parliament Hill.

Royal Commission on the Status of Women appointed.

Order of Canada established to honour distinguished service.

Roland Michener appointed governor general, replacing Georges Vanier.

"O Canada" becomes National Anthem.

EXPO 67 opens in Montreal, April 27; ends October 29: 50.3 million attend.

Navy, army and air force unified into the Canadian Armed Forces.

10,000 dairy farmers snarl Ottawa traffic demanding milk price boost.

Charles de Gaulle fans separatism with "Vive le Quebec libre . . ." speech at Montreal.

Elaine Tanner of Vancouver breaks two world records in swimming at Pan American Games in Winnipeg.